WEB
Publishing for Genealogy

Peter Christian

GENEALOGICAL PUBLISHING Co., Inc.

Second edition © 2000 by Peter Christian.
All rights reserved. No part of this publication
may be reproduced, in any form or by any means,
including electronic reproduction or reproduction
via the Internet, except by permission of the publisher

Published in the USA by Genealogical Publishing Co., Inc.
1001 N. Calvert Street, Baltimore, MD 21202
Library of Congress Catalogue Card Number 99-76711
International Standard Book Number 0-8063-1630-6
Made in the United States of America

Published by arrangement with David Hawgood,
London, England. First edition published 1997.
Web pages from the Society of Genealogists Web site
are copyright © 1999 by the Society of Genealogists,
and are reproduced by permission.

CONTENTS

1. Introduction

The World Wide Web, often simply referred to as the Web, is becoming an increasingly important publishing medium. Not only does it provide an additional means for companies and organizations to publicize their services and activities, but it also offers individuals an ideal way to publish special-interest material that would never find a traditional publisher. As a low-cost medium accessible to millions of readers, it offers great potential for genealogists to publicize their surname interests, the results of their researches, and transcripts of original source materials. The aim of this book is to look at what is involved in publishing your genealogy on the Web, and offer some guidance about how to get started. When you come to actually creating pages, you will need more information about some of the resources and techniques than can be accommodated in these pages. To that end there is a Web site to supplement the material in this book at

http://www.walrus.dircon.co.uk/wpg/

and a § in the text indicates further information is available there.

What Is the World Wide Web?

The World Wide Web is perhaps best thought of as an immense library, made up not of books but of individual **Web pages**, and kept not in one place but all over the world on dedicated computers called **Web servers**. Web pages are read over the Internet by using a piece of software called a **Web browser**. A coherent collection of pages on a single topic or which are the work of a single individual, group or organization is called a **Web site**, usually accessed via a **home page**, a main page which has links to all the other pages on the site.

The reason it's called the Web is that individual pages can be connected in a way that lets the reader follow a link from one page to another: it's a network of interconnected pages that spans the entire Internet.

The key features of the Web that make it different from other publishing media are:

❑ It is a **multimedia** system
It can deal not only with text, but with digitized images (monochrome or color), sound, video, and animation. It can also be used to distribute computer files in any format, making them universally available.

❑ It is a **hypertext** system
Web pages can contain links to other pages. When you select a link on a page (usually by clicking on it with the mouse), the Web browser automatically fetches the page linked to, wherever it is on the Internet. It's as if your library could immediately provide you with a copy of any other book mentioned in whatever you're reading (and turn to the right page for you).

❑ It is a **public access** system
   Although some pages on the Web are restricted to those who belong to a particular organization or have paid some sort of subscription fee, almost all Web pages are accessible to anyone who has access to the Internet.
   Likewise, anyone with his own Internet account can publish material on the Web at no cost. Hundreds of thousands of individuals are publishing on the Web without having to go through traditional publishers or bearing the expense of private printing.

❑ It is a **searchable** system
   There are special facilities on the Web called search engines, which make it possible to find pages on the Web that cover particular subjects or include certain names. Although the indexing and coverage are far from complete, it is still the most comprehensive search system available for any body of general information. And you can immediately view the pages that your search turns up.

❑ It is a **distributed** system
   As long the elements of a Web site are accessible on the Internet, it doesn't matter where the individual parts are physically located. This means that it is easy for groups of people to collaborate on a single "publication" even if they keep their materials on different continents. A good example of this is the UK & Ireland Genealogy Server, GENUKI:[1] to the reader it appears to be a single unified resource, but in fact it involves dozens of collaborators, each making material available on his or her own local Web server.

❑ It is a **dynamic** system
   Information on a Web page can be updated as frequently as the author wishes, so it's easy to ensure that it is always current and as complete as possible. It is easy to add information at any time. This means that a Web site can function as an electronic noticeboard, as well as offer competition to traditional publishing. Also, Web pages can be interactive and readers may be able to use a Web page to submit a surname to a site listing surname interests, for example.

Why Is the Web Useful for Genealogists?

The key features discussed above already suggest some reasons why the Web has great potential for genealogists, but it may be worth looking at some of the particular things that genealogists can do with the Web, and why the Web helps to solve some of the limitations of traditional publishing in genealogy.

Rather than discuss these at length, I have summarized in the tables on page 8 the main points of comparison with traditional genealogical publication.[2]

There are, of course, some disadvantages of Web publishing, such as those given in the second table. But the Web is only a few years old, and some of these problems

---

[1] *http://www.genuki.org.uk/*

[2] See also my article "Genealogical Publishing on the World-Wide Web" in *Computers in Genealogy*, Vol. 5, No. 9 (March 1996), pp. 381–387, for further discussion of these points. The text of this article is on-line at *http://www.sog.org.uk/cig/vol5/509christian.html.*

are already being addressed. It is sometimes argued that not everyone has a computer, and this means the Web is limited in its usefulness. But those without Internet access at home or work can use the facilities in cybercafés and an increasing number of public libraries — it is not necessary to own a computer to *access* the Web any more than it is necessary to own a microfiche reader to use microfiche publications.

All in all, anything you could publish in a book, you can publish on the Web. In addition, the Web has features that make it better than a book for certain genealogical purposes.

What Do You Need for Web Publishing?

One of the reasons for the success of the Web as a publishing medium is that, at a basic level, it requires little in the way of expenditure and little in the way of computing expertise. If you already have an account with an Internet Service Provider (ISP) or with an on-line service such as CompuServe or AOL, you should be able to publish on the Web without additional spending. The following paragraphs look at what you will need.

EQUIPMENT

Apart from a computer and a modem, you will not need any equipment. You do not need a high-performance computer — you can create Web pages on *any* computer. In practical terms, however, it is not a realistic task to try and create Web pages on any computer for which there isn't Web browser software available, as you'll be unable to view what you're creating. This means that you really need a Windows PC or an Apple Macintosh. Most of the specialist software available to help you create Web pages is only available for the PC (running Windows 3.1 or, preferably, Windows 95/98) or Apple Mac. And if you want to use commercial Web publishing software, you will find it expects to run on a fairly well specified computer, including a good-sized hard disk and plenty of memory.

WEB SPACE

You will need an account with an Internet Service Provider that provides you with space to store your pages. Most ISPs include a basic amount of Web space in your subscription, so if you already have Internet access, you shouldn't have to spend more in order to publish your genealogy on the Web. This basic Web space will usually be at least 10MB (megabytes), which is equivalent to about 10 million characters of text, but larger allocations are increasingly common. Some providers even claim to offer "unlimited" Web space. If you are planning to choose an ISP, make sure you get at least 10MB.[3]

If your ISP does not have Web space for subscribers — this is more often the case with services that charge for connection time only, rather than the normal flat-rate, unlimited usage providers — then you should either change your provider or con-

---

[3] The Web sites of ISPs will give you this information. You should be able to find comparative reviews of ISPs in computer magazines

ADVANTAGES OF THE WEB OVER PRINT

For the Web	Against Print
Partial research can be published, then filled out later.	Incomplete material is not easily publishable.
Web search facilities mean the pages can be found by those interested.	With a small print run, it may be difficult for potential readers to hear of or find the publication.
Links facilitate connections between pieces of information; cross-references, even to other sites, are easily followed.	There is no satisfactory way of organizing connected genealogical information in print; cross-references are cumbersome.
Links mean that references to other sources can be kept current, and new ones added.	Reference information goes out-of-date by definition, you cannot refer to subsequently published material.
Any page can be downloaded in seconds from anywhere in the world.	Specialist publications can only be read in specialist libraries or by inter-library loan.
Black & white or color illustrations are equally easy to include.	Color illustrations are prohibitively expensive.
The content of any Web page can be searched interactively.	Material must be indexed if readers are to find information selectively.
Worldwide distribution is automatic, publicity is free.	Distribution and publicity are expensive and/or labor-intensive.
Information can be kept up to date, and corrections of any size made (on a day to day basis, if necessary) at no cost.	Updating information requires a reprint; minor corrections cannot be made economically.
Anyone can publish.	Necessity for a publisher.
There is no stock to be stored, managed or sold.	Money is tied up in stock, which requires storage space and management.

OUTSTANDING PROBLEMS OF WEB PUBLISHING

Against the Web	For Print
Material is available only while the publisher has an Internet account.	Once published, material is available in libraries forever.
The lack of archiving means that published information can be "lost."	Libraries and repositories safeguard published information.
If the publisher changes Internet provider, the address of the material may change.	Bibliographical references are permanent.
There is no quality control.	Editors and publishers guarantee quality.
Charging for access not possible on a non-corporate Internet account.	Existing commercial framework means that anyone can sell material.

sider one of the services that offer free Web space.[4] If you just want to publish your family tree on the Web and no other material, then some genealogical software companies provide free Web space for customers to upload Web pages generated from their products. This is discussed in more detail in Chapter 3.

If your initial allocation is not enough for your needs, Internet providers will sell you additional Web space. This is mostly intended for business and professional users, and tends to be priced accordingly. If you are planning a Web site for a society or a group rather than for personal use, you will need to assess the total space needs and the probable cost. Of course, you can always rent more Web space as and when you need it, and in any case costs are falling all the time. On the whole you are unlikely to need large amounts of space just for personal genealogy or for society and membership information. It's only if you wish to make indexes, transcripts or publications available on-line, or produce high-quality images, that you might need a larger allocation but even so, it will probably take a while to fill 10MB, let alone any larger allocation. [5]

For a society Web site, one thing to watch out for is not the limitation on space, but restrictions on **bandwidth**, i.e. the amount of data downloaded from your Web site. Most ISPs have a limit on this — so many MB per month — and if you're going to have lots of visitors this limit may be exceeded. The ISP will then either close down access to your site temporarily or charge for the excess, so it's important to look at this issue when setting up an account if you expect a high level of traffic on your site.

SOFTWARE

Obviously, you will need software to create the pages, but as long as your computer has a text editor, you already have a basic tool. Your word-processor will certainly have an option to save a document as text (rather than in the word-processor's own proprietary file format), so at worst you could use that. While it is possible to spend several hundred dollars on a sophisticated commercial Web editing tool, it is not necessary — there are freeware and inexpensive shareware Web authoring packages. And for a handful of personal pages, the expense of commercial packages may be overkill. On the other hand, for a substantial site it may be well worth investing in software that provides site maintenance facilities as well as page editing.

If images are going to be part of your Web site, image editing tools will be necessary — even if you're not going to create images from scratch, you will need to crop and resize images, convert to another file format, etc. If you have not already got a suitable painting package, there is very economical shareware that will perform the limited tasks required for Web publishing just as well as fully fledged commercial packages.

---

[4] Angelfire (*http://www.angelfire.com/*) and Geocities (*http://www.geocities.com*) are perhaps the best known of these, but there is an extensive list on Yahoo *http://dir.yahoo.com/Business_and_Economy/Companies/ Internet_Services/Web_Services/Website_Hosting/Free_Web_Pages/*. Usually, your free Web space is "paid for" by carrying advertising, either in a banner on your page or in a floating window.

[5] To put this in perspective: the text of this book would occupy less than 150 KB (kilobytes) as a Web page, i.e. less than 2% of a 10MB allocation, and even with the images it would be unlikely to exceed half a megabyte. Even the entire Society of Genealogists Web site (*http://www.sog.org.uk/*) currently takes up only 13MB.

If you already have an Internet account, you will already have the software needed to connect to it. But you will also need some software to upload your Web pages onto the Web server of your Internet provider. This is normally done with a piece of software called an **FTP client**.[6] If your provider has supplied you with a basic set of Internet software, you will already have this. If not, there are freeware FTP clients which can be downloaded via the Web.§ Some Web authoring software is capable of automating this procedure, as discussed on p. 57.

If you have Internet access, you probably already have a Web browser. But it's a good idea to get a copy of at least one other browser, so that you can see how your pages look with different software. The most popular Web browsers are Netscape Navigator (usually just referred to as Netscape) and Microsoft's Internet Explorer.[7] If you are a Windows or Mac user, you should get copies of both of these, to see how your pages will look to most readers.[8] Both are free of charge, so all it need cost you is download time and disk space.

SKILLS

The skills required to create simple Web pages are not advanced or hard to acquire. This is one of the reasons for the proliferation of material on the Web — it's easy to do. Compared with desktop publishing, or even word-processing, creating a basic Web page is extremely straightforward. Assuming you are already familiar with the Web, and know what sort of features to expect on a Web site, the essentials can be learned in a couple of hours at most. This will be a perfectly satisfactory level of skill for you to be able to publish your genealogical material.

Once you have mastered the basics, however, there are plenty of ways to make your pages more interesting, or to add facilities to your Web site, and some of these will require more advanced skills. But good Web sites are more often the result of having interesting and well-organized material, and a clear purpose, rather than advanced computing expertise. Remember, people will be visiting your genealogy site because you have information, not because you have state-of-the-art special effects.

While you do not need to be a computer expert to create Web pages, there are, nonetheless, certain general computing basics you need to be familiar with before you start. It's helpful if you have some word-processing experience, so that you already have some idea about using a computer for page layout, and it's *essential* that you know how to name and save files on your computer, and have some understanding of how files are organized in directories (DOS and Windows 3.1) or folders (Mac and Windows 95/98). And you will need to be at home with your Web browser,

---

[6] FTP stands for File Transfer Protocol, the standard method of transferring files across the Internet.

[7] According to GVU's survey of May 1998 (*http://www.cc.gatech.edu/gvu/user_surveys/survey-1998-04/reports/1998-04-Technology.html*) 94% of Internet users use one of these two browsers. According to Browserwatch (*http://browserwatch.internet.com/stats/stats.html*), these account for 85% of users, while no other browser for personal computers has more than 3% of users (July 1999).

[8] Unfortunately, pages will not appear identically on Windows and Mac platforms: text appears smaller on the Mac and images brighter, but it's difficult for the amateur Web author to take much account of this.

as you'll be using it all the time to look at your pages as you create them. For this reason, though Web page creation is not complex, it's probably not something you should attempt if you first touched a computer keyboard two days ago.

HELP

This book should contain enough information to give you some idea of what is involved and to get you started, but you will need more information if you're to create more than a basic genealogical Web site. Many of the software tools you can use for creating Web pages will themselves contain help files with a lot of useful material, and this may be all that you require. There are large numbers of books now available on Web page creation, and, of course, the Web itself has thousands of pages of advice and instruction on all aspects of page creation and site design, from the absolute basics to the most abstruse facilities. (See the Appendices.)§

Also, your browser provides an option to look at how a page is constructed (see the next section), so when you see a good design effect on a Web page, you can usually find out how it's done, and adapt it to your own purposes. You can also learn a lot about the design side of Web authoring, simply by looking critically at other people's Web pages and seeing what works well and what doesn't.

How Web Pages Work

Creating Web pages does not really require any technical knowledge. But it is quite useful all the same to have a general idea of how the Web works — this makes it easier to understand how things are done, and why things sometimes don't work. It will also help you understand the technical limitations of the Web, and the impact this has on what counts as good or bad design.

What happens when you view a Web page?

1. *Your browser contacts the server on which the page is held.*

2. *The server responds, saying it's ready for a page request.*

3. *The browser sends the server details of the page it wants.*

4. *The server looks at its files to find the page (if it can't find it, or if it's a page that is not meant for public viewing, it sends an error message).*

5. *The server transmits the text of the page to your computer.*

6. *Your computer receives the page.*

7. *Your browser looks at the page and uses the tags to decide how to display the various bits of text on the page.*

8. *If there are any images on the page, the browser contacts the server again and requests each image in turn (back to step 1 for each image).*

Each Web page is stored on what is called a **Web server**. For your own pages this will be a very fast computer belonging to your Internet provider with enormous amounts of disk space, parceled out between all the subscribers. A large organization, however, may well have its own server (and staff to maintain it). When you access a Web page with your Web browser, the browser contacts the server on which the relevant page is stored, via your Internet connection, and requests the page. The server then responds by transmitting the page to your machine — see the box on previous page for a more detailed description of what happens — or sending an error message saying why it can't fulfill the request. The browser looks at what it receives and turns it into a screen display.

Web pages *look* like a form of desktop publishing but they are in fact created in a completely different way. Rather than being a complex data file, each Web page is simply a plain text file that contains (a) any text that is to be displayed, and (b) special **tags** indicating how the text is to be displayed. Tags are also used to indicate the location of images, and links to other Web pages. Images are not actually stored *in* the pages. Each image on a page is stored as a separate file, and the page contains tags that tell the browser which image files to fetch and display. This is why you can "turn off" the images on your browser — it simply doesn't bother to fetch them. Links, too, are indicated by tags: the **hot spot** is simply tagged with information about which page to fetch when you click on it with the mouse.

Browsers provide a facility for looking at the plain text file that underlies a page. Look for an option with the word "source" in it (in Netscape and Internet Explorer this is on the **View** menu).

The advantage of this way of working is that, as text files, Web pages can be looked at and edited on any type of computer: pages created on one type of computer can be viewed or edited on any other without requiring special file conversion utilities such as are needed to convert between word-processor or desktop publishing formats. Also, it means that you do not need any specific piece of software or even any particular level of hardware to create the pages. As long as a computer has a basic text editor, it can be used to edit pages. Another advantage is that text files are small and can be transmitted very quickly over the Internet, whereas images and word-processor files are much larger, and take correspondingly longer.

The tags used in Web pages indicate how text should look only at a very general level. Rather than specifying, for example, "18 point Optima Bold Italic" for a heading, which would be completely useless for readers without that font installed on their machine, a Web page tag would indicate, say, a "Heading 1" style, and leave it up to the browser to decide which font and point size to use.[9] This is called **logical markup** (or "semantic markup"): the page creator indicates the *function* of a piece of text on the page, rather than describing exactly how it will *look* to the reader (which is **descriptive markup**). When you put "Heading 1" tags around a piece of

---

[9] On text only browsers, such as the lynx browser for the UNIX operating system, the browser has no access to any other fonts, and will use underlining or a different color to indicate the main heading.

text, what you're saying to the browser is, "I don't care how you do it but make sure that this piece of text is the largest heading on the page."

This means that the designer of the Web page specifies the contents of the page, but the browser decides on the presentation.[10] Most browsers allow the user to specify certain defaults, so that if you have poor eyesight or a small screen you can configure your browser to use a larger font size — the page designer doesn't need to do a special "large print" version of the page. Likewise, if you prefer white text on a black background, you, as the reader, can do so, over-riding any color scheme chosen by the page designer. If, for any reason, a browser can't cope with a particular feature it finds on a page, it will do the best it can or simply ignore it, and the content of the page will generally be unaffected.

TAGS AND HTML

Each tag itself consists of a pair of angled brackets containing a special **identifier**, which will be a more or less obvious abbreviation of what the tag does, so, for example, the tag **
** puts a line break in the text. The tags that can be used on Web pages are defined by a **markup language** called **HyperText Markup Language** (HTML).[11] This is an internationally agreed way of marking up material for the Web, and browsers are designed specifically to understand this markup and turn it into a page on screen (in computer terminology, the browser **interprets** the page).

The idea of markup itself is much older than the Web: in traditional typesetting, editors "mark up" the manuscripts sent in by authors to indicate to the typesetter that he should set a particular word in italics, or leave a blank line, or whatever. On the Web, the creator of a page has the editor's job, and the browser is the "typesetter" which follows the markup instructions contained in the page. Your job when designing the page is to mark it up (or get some software to do it for you) so that the browser knows how to "typeset" it. This way of working makes for a very flexible presentation system, in which the reader always gets the best possible display available on his or her system.

Web page design is a rapidly changing field — not only because users have increasingly powerful equipment and Internet connections are improving, but also because designers are demanding additional features to work with. Consequently, HTML is a constantly and rapidly evolving standard. The current standard is HTML 4.0, and all recent browsers should be able to display fully and correctly pages designed to this standard.

HOW PAGES ARE IDENTIFIED

Browsers obviously need to be able to find particular pages. What makes this possible is that each page has a unique identifier called a URL, which stands for **Uni-**

---

[10] Style sheets (see p. 61) allow the page designer to specify layout in detail but keep it separate from the information on the page.

[11] HTML conforms to the SGML (Standard Generalized Markup Language) standard, ISO 8879, which defines a standard for markup languages. HTML is controlled by the World Wide Web Consortium (W3C) on behalf of all Web users and developers. The W3C home page is at *http://www.w3.org/*.

form Resource Locator. In fact, *every* resource on the Internet has its own unique URL. The URL is the "address" of the page on the Internet, specifying

❑ what type of resource it is (whether it's a Web page, a file in an archive, etc.),
❑ the Internet address of the server it's located on,
❑ its location on that server.[12]

For example, the URL for the Web page associated with this book is:

http: // www.walrus.dircon.co.uk / wpg / index.html

type	Server	Directory	file
		= pathname	

The *http:* indicates that it's a Web page,[13] located on the server *www.walrus.dircon.co.uk* (server names are preceded by double slashes), and its pathname on that server is */wpg/index.html*. A pathname is a combination of the filename and the names of the directories or folders in which the file is stored: here the file *index.html* is stored in the directory *wpg* — single slashes separate the elements of the pathname. Note that pathnames are case sensitive: if you type the URL above with *WPG* instead of *wpg* you will get an error message.[14] Server names, on the other hand, are not case sensitive and *WWW.walrus.DIRCON.co.UK* would work just as well.

You will often see URLs that don't give a file name, and end with a slash, or which simply give the name of the server. Whenever the Web server hasn't been asked to send a specific page, it automatically sends the default or home page for the relevant directory. So, for example, you can also access the Web page for this book by going to *http://www.walrus.dircon.co.uk/wpg/* — the Web server knows to send the page *index.html* if no other page in the directory */wpg/* is specified. If the URL contains no pathname at all, the server will send back to the browser the default page for the entire server, so, for example, Microsoft's home page can be specified simply as *http://www.microsoft.com/* without a pathname.

The Process of Web Publishing

Assuming you have your computer, modem, Internet account, and some genealogical information you want to publish, what are the steps necessary to get your material on-line?

---

[12] For a more detailed (and technically more precise) definition, see my *Introduction to URLs* at *http://www.gold.ac.uk/infos/cs/c605.html* .

[13] "http" stands for "HyperText Transfer Protocol," the communications standard which underlies the transmission of Web pages between client and server.

[14] The message will be something like "File not found." You will get this message if a page has changed its URL, but more often it will be due to typing errors. However, some Web servers can automatically detect page requests that are in the wrong case and correct for it.

1. Get some Web editing software and try creating some test pages with a variety of editing tools.

2. Plan your Web site — what is it going to contain, how is it going to be organized?

3. Create the pages on your own computer, viewing them in your browser as you do so, and checking that the links between them work.

4. Connect to your Internet provider and upload all the pages that constitute your Web site to the Web server.

5. Test the pages once they are on the server to make sure they work as intended.

6. Publicize your pages so that people know they exist.

7. Maintain and improve them.

The following chapters look at these steps and some of the issues involved.

2. Web Publishing Software

Unlike most computer tasks, Web page creation can be carried out with any one of a wide range of software tools, from basic text editors to sophisticated Web site management systems. In this chapter, I will look at the different types of software available. Tools that are specifically designed for genealogical use and facilities for creating Web pages directly from genealogical software are discussed in the following chapter.

Whereas there are only a handful of competitors for the title of best word-processor, there are dozens of competing Web authoring tools, and the range is growing all the time.[15] The field of Web publishing is developing very rapidly, and new software is becoming available all the time, not just new packages but often new types of software tools.

The general tools available for Web authoring can be classified in two main ways. Firstly, there is a distinction between editors and WYSIWYG ("what you see is what you get") applications. With an editor, you type in the tags yourself, whereas a WYSIWYG application is like a word-processor — you take care of the appearance of the page and the software works out what tags are needed. Secondly, there is a distinction between general-purpose software, such as a word-processor, and applications that have been specifically designed for Web authoring. The following sections look at the merits of each type of software and draw attention to some of their limitations.

Text Editors

Because HTML files are plain text files, they can be created perfectly satisfactorily with a text editor such as the Windows Notepad or even the DOS Edit program. Many Web page designers in fact prefer to use an editor rather than any more sophisticated tool, because it provides more precise control over the content of the page. For the beginner, it also means you don't need to learn how to use a new piece of software. However, some features, such as tables, can be extremely laborious to create "by hand" with an editor, and the major disincentive for the beginner is that you actually need to know which tags to use and how to use them. Against this is the long-term advantage that using an editor gives you a much better understanding of how Web pages work.

The basic editor that comes with your computer is in principle perfectly adequate for Web authoring, though the facilities of Notepad, for example, are rather restricting for creating more than a couple of pages. However, there are also freeware and shareware editors available, which can provide more sophisticated editing facilities,

---

[15] TUCOWS (*http://www.tucows.com/*) has over 50 pieces of general Web authoring shareware available for Windows 95/98, and well over 60 tools for specific tasks.

and many now have some support for Web authoring, even though they are general-purpose editors.[16]

Obviously a text editor will not provide facilities for viewing the Web pages you are editing. However, once you have saved a page to disk, you will be able to use your Web browser to view it, since all Web browsers allow you to look at a Web page stored on your hard disk as well as pages on the Web. Also, you can use the browser's Refresh or Reload feature to update the view of the page each time you save the changes to disk from the editor.

HTML Editors

An HTML editor is an editor that has some special functions specific to Web editing. The method of creating pages — typing in the text and tags — is the same as with a standard editor, but you can also expect to find at the very least a button bar for the insertion of common tags, and HTML reference materials. And there may be more sophisticated features, such as automated table creation, a color palette, error checking, and even site management tools, which will check that the links between your pages are sound. Some HTML editors have built-in page viewing facilities, but most are or can be configured to call up your browser automatically when you ask to preview a page you are working on.

The advantage of this type of tool over a standard editor is that it gives you all the flexibility of a text editor but will provide a number of labor-saving shortcuts for the creation of Web pages.

Word-Processors and Other Applications

The need for Web editing is now so considerable that almost all recent versions of software used in document creation, including word-processors, desktop publishers, databases, etc., include Web publishing facilities as standard.

The advantage of using a word-processor rather than an editor to create Web pages is that while you still need to have general familiarity with the typical components of a Web page, you do not actually need to remember the tags and how to use them correctly. Also, of course, this is by far the easiest way to convert existing word-processed documents into Web pages: you simply open the file, and you can immediately save it as a Web page, without further ado.

Unfortunately, these are not always entirely satisfactory tools, for two reasons. Firstly, they may make decisions for you about certain aspects of the page which may be hard to alter; Microsoft Word 97, for example, insists on converting headings into precise font information rather than into HTML's general-purpose heading tags. Also, word-processors inevitably lag behind HTML developments and may not be able to

---

[16] For Windows users, TextPad (*http://www.textpad.com/*) is highly recommended; the favorite of Macintosh Web authors is BBEdit (*http://www.barebones.com/*).

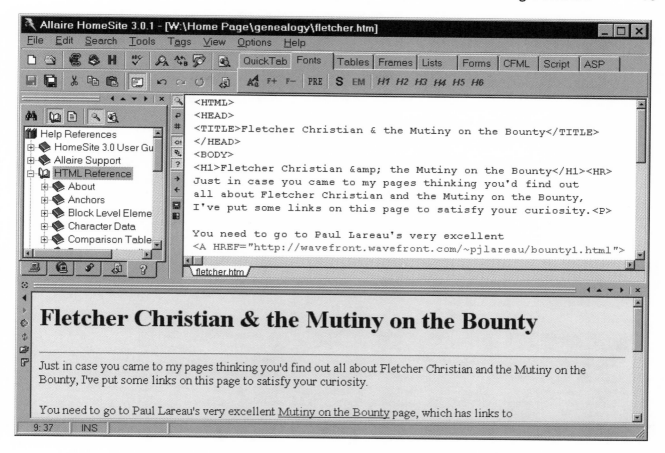

Fig. 1: An HTML Editor

This is a screenshot from Allaire's HomeSite 3.0 (*http://www.allaire.com/*), a highly regarded commercial HTML editor. In addition to the main editing window top right, you can see the page preview window at the bottom and the on-line help index on the left. The button bar provides quick access to tags in various categories. You can see the whole page at *http://homepages.gold.ac.uk/peter/genealogy/fletcher.htm*.

cope with all the features in the current standard and supported by the latest browsers. Still, as a quick way of preparing existing documents for the Web, these tools can be very useful.

A word-processor may seem the obvious general-purpose tool for Web authoring, but if you have data stored in a recent version of one of the main spreadsheet or database programs, you should find you are able to create Web pages from these, too. This means you can create pages of parish register entries, indexes, etc. directly from your database or spreadsheet (see Fig. 2). Naturally, these tend to be more limited in their Web facilities than word-processors and are really intended only for highly structured information such as tables rather than for general page layout, so you will probably want to edit pages subsequently in a word-processor or HTML editor to improve their appearance.

WYSIWYG Web Authoring Tools

Since word-processors are designed as general-purpose document editing tools, they are not really ideal for the creation of Web pages. For this you need to look at the WYSIWYG Web authoring tools, which can be regarded as special-purpose word-processors. As with a word-processor, you worry about the design and content of your pages, and leave the software to worry about the tags.

They may allow for the complete management of Web sites, ensuring that pages have a common look, as well as providing support for some advanced features that novice users would not easily be able to create with an editor. In many cases they provide "wizards," which take you step by step through the process of creating pages. They also tend to make using images easier, and they often include facilities to automate the process of uploading pages to your Web server.

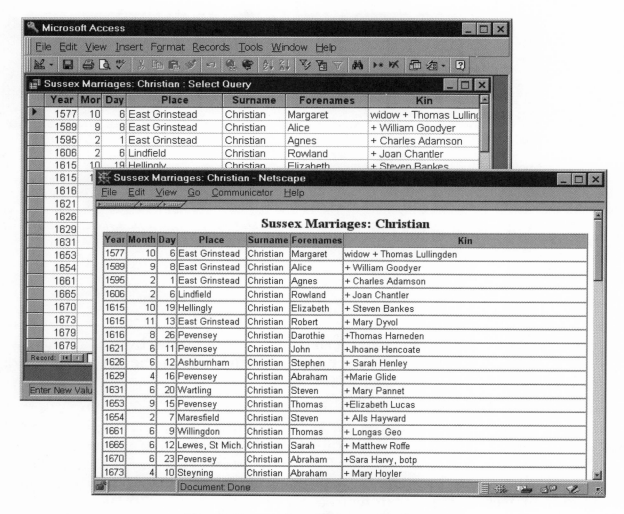

Fig. 2: From Database to Web Page

Behind is a database query (find all the Christian marriages in Sussex) run in an Access97 database. In front is the Web page that was created via Access's "Save as HTML" feature.

Some of these tools are primarily designed to simplify Web publishing for novices, while others are intended to supply every possible need of the professional Web author. Some of the main commercial packages are as follows:

❏ Adobe PageMill,
❏ Macromedia Dreamweaver,
❏ Microsoft FrontPage

These are all available for both Windows 95/98 and the Macintosh — you will probably not find software of this sort for other systems or for Windows 3.1. It is not possible here to give an overview of all the packages available, and new ones are appearing all the time. Demo versions are available for the three listed, so you can try them out first, and you should be able to find in-depth reviews in computer magazines or on-line.§

While the programs mentioned above are commercial software, there are a number of shareware packages, and four that are completely free:

❏ Netscape Composer (part of Netscape Communicator 4.0 and above)
❏ Microsoft FrontPage Express (part of Internet Explorer 4.0 and above)
❏ CompuServe's Home Page Wizard
❏ AOLPress§

If you use Netscape Communicator as your browser, you will find that you already have Composer (on Netscape's **Window** menu), and there's a similar tool in Netscape 3.0 Gold. FrontPage Express will be available if you do a full install of Internet Explorer.

Of the four, the Home Page Wizard is the least satisfactory. While very simple to use, it has a very limited range of facilities, and has the severe drawback that it stores pages in a proprietary format, only converting them to HTML when you publish them. Likewise, it cannot be used to edit existing HTML pages. This means that you cannot easily use this package in combination with another — a rather bizarre approach when you consider that the whole point of HTML is that it's not tied to a particular type of computer or to specific software. On the other hand, the others, while they have their limitations, are quite good basic Web authoring programs. They may lack the advanced features of something like FrontPage, but for a personal Web site, perhaps used in combination with a good editor, these should certainly meet most needs.

HTML Converters

If you have an older word-processor without built-in Web publishing facilities, you may still be able to use it for Web publishing. There are a wide range of **HTML converters** (also called **filters**), which will convert files to Web page format. Needless to say, the converters can only convert what they find, and can't be used to edit the converted page. You will almost certainly need to tidy up converted pages with some other sort of editor, and obviously converted documents won't contain Web-specific features such as links. But an appropriate converter used in conjunction with another editing tool could save you a lot of time in preparing existing material for the Web, and there are freeware converters for a wide variety of file formats (not just for word-processors).§

In the early days of the Web, these converters were important because at that time almost no major software package supported Web authoring. Nowadays, you are only likely to need a converter if you are using older software.

In fact, you may not need a converter: even if your database or spreadsheet software does not have a facility for creating Web pages, there are other methods of converting this material as long as your word-processor can create Web pages:

❏ Use mailmerge to get data from your database or spreadsheet into a word-processed document and then save it as a Web page

❏ Save data or reports in a format that can be imported into your word-processor — RTF is recommended, since this preserves formatting information

Other File Formats

In fact, you can save data from almost any program so that it is viewable on the Web, without a converter, as browsers are not restricted to displaying Web pages. As you can see from Figs. 7 and 8 (p. 33), they can display plain text files. This means that if you already have material in plain text format, you can simply put it on your Web site and people will be able to read it. Of course, it will look rather boring, and it won't have Web-specific features like links, but if it contains useful information, this will be better than nothing. And it also means that no matter how ancient your word-processor or database you will be able to put material on the Web as long as you can save it as ASCII text.

But Web browsers can in fact deal with *any* type of file. If the browser finds a file it does not know how to deal with, it will offer you two main options:

❏ Save to disk so that you can look at the file by using another piece of software

❏ Tell it which software to use to display the file

Browsers can be configured to call up particular software to display particular types of file, so, for example, you could tell your browser that it should automatically start Microsoft Word whenever it comes across a file with the extension *.doc*. In fact this is precisely how Web browsers deal with sound and video — they do not have these facilities built-in, but they look for "helper applications" to call up when they come across sound or video files. This extensibility is one of the key features that provide future-proofing for the Web — browsers can cope with *any* file format, even ones that haven't been invented yet.

There are, however, two issues which you need to consider when providing files that your readers are going to download rather than read on-line: file format and file size.

While HTML and the graphics formats used on the Web are standard (and can be handled by any type of computer), if you make, say, a word-processor file available for downloading, you will need to consider making it available in a format that all your readers can deal with, whatever hardware and software they have. For word-processor files, a common solution is to save in RTF format, which is one that can be created and read by all major word-processors and is not tied to any particular make of computer. For database files, dBase and CSV are formats that can be read by any commercial database software, while for spreadsheets standard formats are Lotus 1-2-3 and Excel.

You will notice that word-processor, database, and spreadsheet files tend to be larger than text files. For this reason, it is usual to **compress** files that you are making available for downloading. In fact, this is often done even with text files, such as GEDCOM files. Compressed files are usually at least 20%–30% smaller than the original file, and can be as much as 70% smaller. This represents a significant reduction in the time it takes to download them, and, of course, compressed files also take up less Web space.

A further advantage of compression is that it allows you to collect many different files into a single compressed file (often called an **archive**). This makes it easy to ensure that a reader downloads all of a group of files that belong together, and so is the normal way of providing software, for example. If you wanted readers to be able to download your PAF (Personal Ancestral File) Family Records data — which is stored in several different files — you would compress all the files into a single archive. In order to compress files, you will need an appropriate **archiver** for your computer.§

When you make a file available on your Web site, you provide access to it simply by including a link to it on a page. It is also helpful to tell your readers what format the file is in and the file size.

Finally, there is one format that will allow *any* file to be viewable on the Web as long as it comes from an application that can print. **Adobe Acrobat** is an application that can turn a PostScript file — this is what your computer sends to a PostScript printer — into a document in Adobe's **Portable Document Format** (PDF). With the Acrobat software installed on your computer, you can create a PDF file simply by selecting the Acrobat PDFWriter as your "printer" and printing to it just as if it were a physical printer.

In order to be able to view a PDF file on the Web, you need to download and install Adobe's Acrobat Reader, which is free of charge. While the Web in general shuns proprietary data formats, PDF is quite widely used. It has the particular advantages of reproducing accurately a document intended for printing, and of being immune to alteration — you cannot make changes in an existing PDF document, even with the PDF writing software. The disadvantage, of course, if you want to use PDF on your Web site, is that you will have to purchase a copy of the software that creates PDF files, and your visitors will need to have the viewer installed.

The main use of PDF on the Web is for making long reports available in their original page layout in a format not tied to any particular word-processor, and I have not yet seen PDF used on a genealogical Web site. However, if you have the Acrobat viewer installed, you can see an EasyTree pedigree chart in this format at *http://www.walrus.dircon.co.uk/wpg/figures/fwm.pdf*.

Other Utilities

Alongside the basic tools you use to create your pages, there are other tools that you may find useful, though you may find that some of these are actually included in your Web authoring software, particularly if it's a commercial package.

GRAPHICS EDITORS

Even if you aren't intending to create your own images for your Web pages, you will need a basic graphics editor in order to

❏ convert images to the required format,
❏ crop or scale images,
❏ reduce the number of colors.

If you want to do more advanced image manipulation, you will need a more sophisticated graphics program.

COLOR PICKERS

If you are using an editor, then, because of the way colors are specified in HTML (see p. 40), it's useful to have a tool that tells you the markup required to achieve a particular color or set of colors. You should find that WYSIWYG Web authoring tools have this sort of facility built in.§

PAGE CHECKERS

It is very useful, especially when you first start designing Web pages, to have some way of checking them for errors. This is particularly true if you are creating pages with an editor rather than a word-processor or a Web authoring package (which will normally not allow pages to be created with errors).[17] A downloadable tool that does this is the shareware CSE 3310 HTML Validator,[18] but there are a number of HTML **validators** that can be used interactively on the Web to check a page once it is accessible on a Web server.§

LINK CHECKERS

It is also useful to have a tool that will check that your links are correct. There are two reasons for this. Firstly, when designing a site, it is useful to be able to check the links between your pages; secondly, if you have links from your site to other Web pages elsewhere, you need to check periodically that these links are still valid.

For the first purpose, it is best to have software that will do this on your own computer so that you can correct links before you upload pages to the server, and Web authoring software increasingly does this. Software that does not actually check links may well allow you to create internal links via drag and drop or via a file menu, which guarantees that a link points to the correct file. For checking external links you will need to use an on-line link checker.[19]

Which Is the Best Tool?

The best tool is one that has the features you need and that you find easiest to use. Initially, it's worth trying to create a simple page with a text editor in any case, just

---

[17] However, Microsoft Word 97 frequently introduces HTML errors into pages it converts.

[18] *http://www.htmlvalidator.com/*

[19] For example, Xenu, available from *http://www.snafu.de/~tilman/xenulink.html*

2. Web Publishing Software   25

to get some understanding of how Web pages work. If your word-processor supports Web authoring, then you can also try out its capabilities. Likewise, if you use the latest version of Netscape Communicator or Internet Explorer, you should try the Web authoring facilities. As you get more experienced, you may want to try out some of the other tools, especially the HTML editors.

Remember: because Web pages are stored in a standard, non-proprietary format, you can freely switch between editing tools and you are not tied in to a particular piece of software.[20]

While the range of tools available can be rather daunting, they are regularly reviewed in computer magazines. There are many on-line-reviews, and some software archives, such as TUCOWS, give ratings which will make it easier to decide which to try.[21]

---

[20] There are *some* limitations: if you add by hand tags that are not supported by a particular HTML editor or word-processor, you may not be able to edit these tags using the program.

[21] Overviews of the main tools available: TERENA's Guide to Network Resource Tools (*http://www.terena.nl/libr/gnrt/providing/authoring-clients.html*); a brief comparative feature list of WYSIWYG editors: *http://www.mailbase.ac.uk/lists/web-support/1998-07/0025.html*

3. Genealogical Tools

There is one thing the tools discussed in the previous chapter cannot do: turn material stored in a family history database into Web pages to produce an on-line tree. For this you are going to need to take your family tree package as the starting point and choose one of three options:

❑ If you use genealogy software that has facilities for outputting Web pages, then you will be able to create the pages directly from the program.

❑ No matter what genealogy software you are using, it should be able to save the data in GEDCOM format, and you will be able to use a converter to turn the GEDCOM file into a set of Web pages.

❑ Otherwise, your genealogy program may be able to save reports in some other format that you can then convert to HTML.

This chapter will look at these options in turn.

Genealogy Software with Web Output

Just as word-processors and other applications now include Web authoring facilities, so general genealogy packages can increasingly be used to create Web pages for genealogical information as an essential option. At the time of writing, the latest versions of the following genealogy packages had Web publishing facilities: §

❑ Ancestral Quest
❑ Family Matters
❑ Family Origins
❑ Family Tree Maker
❑ Generations

❑ The Master Genealogist
❑ Personal Ancestral File for Windows
❑ Reunion
❑ Ultimate Family Tree
❑ Win-Family

A number of software companies provide a Web site where customers can upload Web pages generated by their software. This is the case with Ultimate Family Tree, Family Origins, and Family Tree Maker, for example.[22]

Exactly what these packages produce in the way of Web pages is very variable: Family Matters produces a series of family group reports, with an index of individuals (see Fig. 4), while Ultimate Family Tree produces a register report for each surname with an index of surnames and individuals (see Fig. 3). And it should not be assumed that these programs will make other approaches redundant, since some can deal only with material for the descendants/ancestors of a particular individual and not the entire database.

---

[22] Family Tree Maker will *only* create a set of pages for uploading to the FTM Web site — there is no option to save to your hard disk or upload to another site.

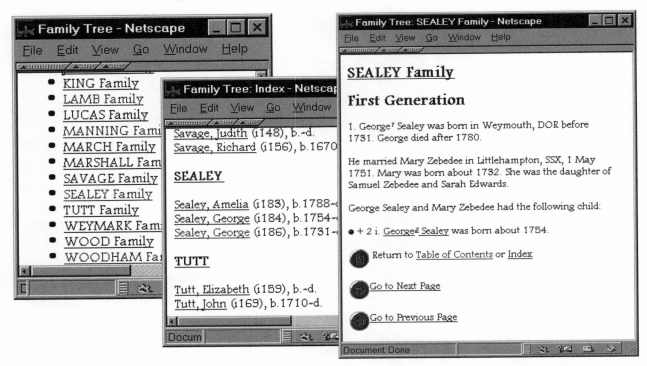

Fig. 3: Web Pages Created by Ultimate Family Tree

GEDCOM Conversion Tools

Using a GEDCOM converter is in some ways the easiest solution, since it does not matter which genealogical package you use, as long as it has a GEDCOM export facility. Although you can edit pages after they have been through a converter, converters tend to produce a large number of fairly small pages, with many links between them. It is better to control the content by selecting the information to be included in the GEDCOM file and configuring the converter beforehand, as subsequent editing could be a major task.

There is an increasing number of GEDCOM converters. The first and probably best known is Gene Stark's GED2HTML, which is available as shareware for Windows, Mac and UNIX systems. This program takes a GEDCOM file and turns it into a group of Web pages containing:

- ❏ a set of pages with an entry for each individual, with notes, and with links to spouses, children, ancestors and source references (see Fig. 5);
- ❏ an index of individuals, with links to the relevant entries for individuals;
- ❏ an index of surnames, with links to the index of individuals;
- ❏ a page containing the details of sources referred to;
- ❏ a text file containing details of all included individuals, in the format required by the GENDEX project (see p. 58).

As you can see from Fig. 5, the ancestors are arranged in a tree format, and all individuals mentioned have links to their own pages. Source references (in square brackets) link to a sources page.

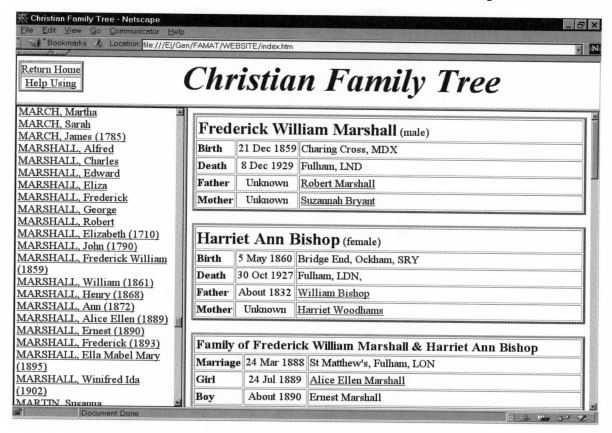

Fig. 4: Web Pages Created by Family Matters

Note the use of frames for a permanent heading and the scrolling list of individuals — clicking on a name brings up the family group record in the right-hand panel.

There is a range of options to control various aspects of the pages created by GED2HTML. For example, you can specify how many generations of ancestors are to be included on each individual's entry, which can make a big difference to the amount of Web space needed for the pages.

While GED2HTML may be the best known, there are several alternatives with a range of different types of output. These programs also vary as to whether

- ❏ notes and sources are or can be included,
- ❏ information on living individuals can be removed,
- ❏ a GENDEX file is produced (see p. 58),
- ❏ baptism and burial information is or can be included,
- ❏ the pages created can be customized during the generation process,
- ❏ the number of individuals or family groups on each Web page can be modified.

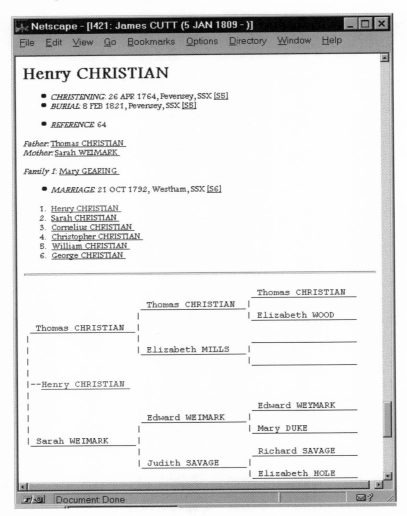

Fig. 5: A Family Group Sheet from GED2HTML

Unfortunately baptism and burial dates, while they can be included in family group reports, are usually not substituted for missing birth or death dates in the index of individuals, who are therefore listed without dates. Many GEDCOM converters do not provide for baptism and burial at all.

Several of these programs are freeware, while the remainder are shareware with registration fees mostly of $20 or under. With the exception of HTMLGenie, the unregistered version of which only works with its own sample data, all of these can be evaluated with your own GEDCOM before registration.

A comparative table listing 20 GEDCOM converters is given opposite.

GEDCOM to HTML Conversion Software

	License	System	Types of Output	Bapt/Bur	Sources	Notes	Privacy	Gendex	Remarks/Limitations
Familia	Free	Win	desc	✗	✗	✗	✗	✗	requires Family Tree Maker
GED2HTM	free	DOS	ped	✗	✗	✗	✗	✗	
GED2HTML	$20	Win, UNIX	ind ped	✔	✔	✔	✔	✔	
GED2WEB	free	Win	fgr ped desc	✔	✗	✔	✗	✔	
GED2WWW	free	DOS	fgr	✗	✗	✗	✔	✔	no customization
GED4WEB	$15	Win		✗	✔	✔	✔	✗	
GedcomToHTML	free	UNIX	ind	bur	✗	✔	✔	✗	requires PERL
GedHTree	$14.95	Win	fgr ped desc	✗	✗	✔	✔	✗	max. 14 generations unreg.
GedPage	$10	Win	fgr	✗	✔	✔	✗	✔	limited customization
GEDTable	free	Win	ind	✗	✗	✗	✗	✗	viewable with IE4 only
GenDesigner	$29.95	Win	ind ped	✔	✗	✔	✗	✗	
HTML Genie	$19.95	Win	fgr reg desc ped	✔	✗	✔	✔	✔	demo only works with sample database
JavaGED	$20	any	fgr ped desc	✗	✔	✔	✔	✔	uses Java
Kinship Archivist	$20	Win	ind, family pages	✔	✗	✔	✔	✗	limited screen modes; family page doesn't show surname
PAF2HTM	free	DOS	ped	✗	✗	✗	✗	✗	Converts PAF data directly
Rootsview	$29	Win	fgr	✗	✗	✔	✔	✗	
Sparrowhawk	$20	Mac	fgr ped	✔	✔	✔	✔	✔	Mac version of GED2HTML
Ufti	free/$20	Win	fgr ped	✔	✔	✔	✔	✔	
Webbit	free	DOS	fgr	✗	✗	✔	✗	✔	Requires Qbasic
webGED Progenitor	$20	Win	fgr ped desc	✔	✗	✔	✔	✔	uses Java

Key to Output	desc=descendant chart fgr=family group record ind=individual record ped=pedigree chart reg=register report
Key to Columns	gendex=creates gendex file (see p. 58) privacy=removes living persons bapt/bur=includes baptism & burial data sources=includes sources notes=includes notes

These details were correct as far as possible at the time of writing, but most of these programs are still being developed by their authors and additional features may be found in current versions.

Familia	http://thor.prohosting.com/~nssd/index.html
GED2HTM	http://table.jps.net~johns1/
GED2HTML	http://www.gendex.com/
GED2WEB	http://www.oramwt.demon.co.uk/GED2WEB/ged2web.htm
GED2WWW	http://www.netcom.com/~lhoward/ged2www.html
GED4WEB	http://www.ged4web.com/
gedcomToHTML	http://www.bath.ac.uk/~enpdp/Gedcom/gedcomToHTML.html
GedHTree	http:// http://www.users.uswest.net/~gwel/gedhtree.htm
GedPage	http://www.fronteirnet.net/~rjacob/grdpsge.htm
GEDTable	http://www.cobnet.com/Programs/GEDTable/
GenDesigner	http://www.gendesigner.com/
HTMLGenie	http://www.geneaware.com
JavaGED	http://www.sc3.net/JavaGEDHome.html
Kinship Archivist	http://kinshiparchivist.com/
PAF2HTM	http://table.jps.net/~johns1/
Rootsview	http://home.earthlink.net/~naturalsoft/rootsview.htm
Sparrowhawk	http://www.bradankathy.com/genealogy/sparrowhawk.html
Ufti	http://www.ufti.com/
Webbit	http://ourworld.compuserve.com/homepages/Kreibaum/credits.htm
webGED Progenitor	http://www.access.digex.net/~giammot/webged/

Examples of the pages created by these programs will normally be found at the relevant Web site and Mark Knight has examples of many of them, all created from the same GEDCOM file at http://help.surnameweb.org/knight/.

Genealogy Software without Web Facilities

If your current genealogy package does not itself provide HTML output, you should still be able to turn your package's reports into Web pages, without necessarily using a GEDCOM converter. Indeed, other ways of creating Web pages could be useful even if your genealogy software *has* Web publishing facilities, as these are often restricted to a single form of output, i.e. a set of linked pages for a single line of descent, or for the ancestors of an individual, whereas ideally it would be possible to turn any report into a Web page or pages.

Exactly how you do this will depend on a number of factors: the sort of computer you are using; your genealogy package's reporting/printing/exporting facilities; the type of report or export option you are using; and your Web editing software. This means it is only possible to give general guidelines here and not specific instructions.

This pedigree chart (here reduced to about half the actual size) was created in EasyChart (the charting program that comes with Generations), and saved in Windows Metafile Format. It was then pasted into a Microsoft Word document. When that document was saved as an HTML file, the image was automatically converted to a GIF file (of about 20KB).

A certain amount of experimentation was needed in EasyChart to get the image to a suitable size, as subsequent resizing of graphics can cause legibility problems with any text they contain.

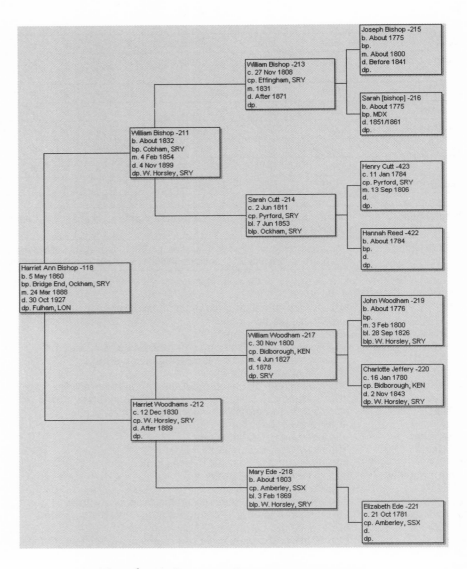

Fig. 6: Pedigree Chart as GIF Image

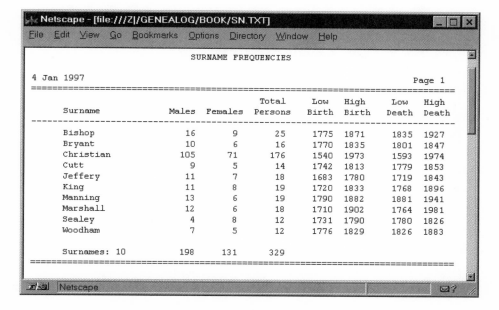

```
Netscape - [file:///Z|/GENEALOG/Book/Wb_dr.htm]
File  Edit  View  Go  Bookmarks  Options  Directory  Window  Help

William Bishop - 213 (c.27 Nov 1808 - After 1871) & Sarah Cutt - 214 (c.2 Jun 1811 - bl.7
|    William Bishop - 211 (About 1832 - 4 Nov 1899) & Harriet Woodhams - 212 (c.12 Dec 18
|    |    William Bishop - 408 (c.14 Jan 1855 - )
|    |    Ellen Bishop - 407 (c.24 Feb 1856 - )
|    |    James Bishop - 406 (c.30 Aug 1857 - )
|    |    Alice Mary Bishop - 405 (c.26 Dec 1858 - )
|    |    Harriet Ann Bishop - 118 (5 May 1860 - 30 Oct 1927) & Frederick William Marshal
|    |    |    Alice Ellen Marshall - 114 (24 Jul 1889 - 1972) & Henry J Lambert - 243 (
|    |    |    Ernest Marshall - 128 (About 1890 - About 1892)
|    |    |    Frederick Marshall - 129 (About 1893 - 1914)
|    |    |    Ella Mabel Mary Marshall - 130 (28 Nov 1895 - 22 Sep 1977) & Walter Henry
|    |    |    Winifred Ida Marshall - 122 (26 Nov 1902 - 24 Oct 1981) & Peter Godfrey Ch
|    |    Edward Bishop - 404 (c.2 Feb 1862 - )
|    |    Frederick Bishop - 403 (c.20 Mar 1864 - )
|    |    George Bishop - 402 (c.3 Dec 1865 - )
|    |    Samuel Bishop - 401 (c.14 Jul 1867 - )
|    |    Lucy Kate Bishop - 400 (c.5 Nov 1871 - bl.23 Dec 1872)
|    Henry Bishop - 432 (30 Jun 1836 - )
|    Job Bishop - 431 (22 Oct 1838 - bl.5 Aug 1846)
|    Harriet Bishop - 430 (26 Mar 1841 - )
|    Charles Bishop - 429 (26 Jan 1844 - )
|    John Bishop - 428 (6 Aug 1846 - )
|    Isaac Bishop - 427 (c.1 Apr 1849 - bl.26 Dec 1850)
|    Ruth Bishop - 424 (About 1849 - After 1871)
|    Lydia Bishop - 426 (c.7 Sep 1851 - )
|    Sarah Bishop - 425 (c.3 Jul 1853 - bl.24 Aug 1853)

Document Done
```

Fig. 7: Indented Descendants Chart from RTF File

This indented descendants chart originated in Reunion, from which it was saved to disk in RTF format. It was imported into WordPerfect. It could have been saved unchanged as a plain text file, but in this case, the essential HTML tags were typed in before the file was saved as an ASCII text file.

Normally, the browser will collapse multiple spaces and wrap lines that run off the edge of the screen. When you are importing text where the original layout needs to be preserved, as here, you can achieve this by putting it between **<PRE>** ... **</PRE>** tags. The browser will use a monospaced font (e.g. Courier) for such text.

To produce this page, the PAF (for DOS) printer was changed to "DOS text printer." Then the "Select Printing Option" (in Forms & Reports) was changed to "Print to Disk File" and a file name chosen. When the report was selected, it was automatically created on disk rather than sent to the printer. The plain text file can be displayed by a browser without modification.

```
Netscape - [file:///Z|/GENEALOG/BOOK/SN.TXT]
File  Edit  View  Go  Bookmarks  Options  Directory  Window  Help

                          SURNAME FREQUENCIES
4 Jan 1997                                                     Page 1
=====================================================================
                                    Total   Low    High   Low    High
        Surname   Males  Females  Persons  Birth  Birth  Death  Death
        -------------------------------------------------------------
        Bishop       16       9       25    1775   1871   1835   1927
        Bryant       10       6       16    1770   1835   1801   1847
        Christian   105      71      176    1540   1973   1593   1974
        Cutt          9       5       14    1742   1813   1779   1853
        Jeffery      11       7       18    1683   1780   1719   1843
        King         11       8       19    1720   1833   1768   1896
        Manning      13       6       19    1790   1882   1881   1941
        Marshall     12       6       18    1710   1902   1764   1981
        Sealey        4       8       12    1731   1790   1780   1826
        Woodham       7       5       12    1776   1829   1826   1883

        Surnames: 10  198     131      329
=====================================================================

Netscape
```

**Fig. 8: A Surname Frequency List "Printed" by
Personal Ancestral File 2.1**

If your package has a facility to export data to a file in a word-processor format — for example, Generations can save reports in both Word and RTF formats — then it should be a simple matter to convert the output to a Web page. If this does not seem to be possible, you should be able to get the data printed to a text file rather than to the printer. This may be an option within your genealogy package (as with Personal Ancestral File) or it may need to be set up as a general option on your computer as a whole (as for any Windows software, for example). If you can select from a range of printers, choose one that looks as if it will produce plain text output without any printer control codes (something like "generic text printer" or "ASCII printer"). You will need to consult your documentation to see how to do this for your computer or software.

4. Designing Your Web Site

What to Include

Before you start designing your Web site, you need to consider what the aim of the site is: who is it for, and what will it contain? What you decide to include on your Web pages will depend on

- ❏ what information you have,
- ❏ what function you want your pages to fulfill,
- ❏ how much Web space you have available,
- ❏ how much time you intend to devote to it.

For example, if you are involved in a one-name study you will have a different view from someone running a family history society site. The last item in this list may not seem like a design decision at all, but will be important for a society site — a list of forthcoming events that is out-of-date because you haven't had time to update it will not be good PR. It's better to start with a small site and add to it as you gain experience and find the time.

Organizing Your Information

If people come to your Web site expecting to find genealogical information, it is up to you to design your pages so that they can

- ❏ see what information you provide,
- ❏ easily access the particular information they might be interested in,
- ❏ find out how to get in touch with you.

It is best to think about what you will be providing and how best to organize it *before* you start creating pages in earnest. Reorganizing a hastily thrown together Web site can be a very time-consuming and tedious job. Initial planning is probably better done with pen and paper than with the computer.

Your basic tools for organization are

- ❏ the Web **page** itself,
- ❏ **links** between pages,
- ❏ the **layout** features on the page.

One of the best ways to learn what works and what doesn't is to look critically at other material on the Web. And one thing is very easy to forget: when you are creating pages on your own computer, they will always be loaded by your browser *much* faster from your own hard disk than they will load for someone accessing your pages from a distant server via a phone line and a modem.

THE PAGE

Each page should be a unit of information, complete unto itself. Think of it as an encyclopedia entry: it should make sense in its own right, even if it has lots of cross references to other information. Splitting up your information into sensible and manageable units is the first basic design task in Web authoring: too many small pages and your readers will be endlessly flitting from page to page; a small number of very large pages, and readers will either not bother to scroll down to the bottom, or the pages will take so long to download that readers will give up. Not more than five or six screenfuls to one page is a good rule of thumb. And if there's a good reason why you *must* have a long page make sure there are good headings and aids to navigation (see, for example, Fig. 15, p. 53).

With a large document, consider splitting it into parts rather than leaving it as one long page, if this makes it more manageable. If, for example, you have a long surname index, few readers will want the whole page, especially if it's going to take five minutes to download — they'll just want to go quickly to the parts of the alphabet with surnames of interest to them.

There are also certain pieces of information the page should always contain:

- ❏ a title
- ❏ a main heading at the top indicating the content
- ❏ the name of the person responsible for the page, preferably accompanied by an e-mail address (traditionally this goes at the bottom of the page)

While this might not seem necessary for any but your Home Page, readers will not always come to your site via the Home Page. Also, the title is a good idea for every page, because if a reader bookmarks a page, the title will help identify your page among all the other bookmarks.[23] Likewise on any printout, headings and a title will indicate where the page comes from and what it shows.

If you are providing what is meant to be up-to-date information, it's also useful to put the date the page was last edited. This is helpful for readers because it allows them to judge how current the information is; it also helps you spot pages that may need checking. It can also be useful to have a way of indicating when any part of the site has been updated. This is usually done via a "What's New" page, which again helps you by reminding you what you did to the site when.[24]

LINKS

Links fulfill two quite different functions. Firstly, they are the glue that hold your Web site together, making it possible to get from one page to another. Secondly, they can provide connections to other Web sites of related interest.

If you have only a small number of pages, you can simply have a link from your Home Page to each other page on your site. But with more pages, it's better to organize them hierarchically. Break your information down into separate topics or areas, and give

---

[23] This is Netscape's terminology; in Internet Explorer this list of sites to remember is called Favorites.

[24] See, for example, the Society of Genealogists' "What's New" page at *http://www.sog.org.uk/new.html*.

each topic its own main page. You can then provide a link to each topic from the Home Page, while the topic pages provide the links to the individual pages with information. If you do have a lot of links on a particular page, try and group them under headings, so the reader can see what sort of information they link to.

For example, if you're researching several lines of ancestry, you might have a main page for each surname. If you're concentrating on a single family, you might have separate areas for narrative, documents, and family tree, and you can further subdivide within those topics. You might, of course, have interests outside genealogy and so have other material on your Web site. In that case your Home Page would provide an entry point to each different area, and your main genealogy page would be at the second level.

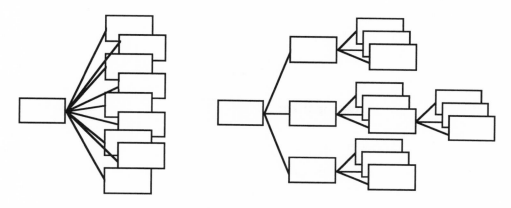

Fig. 9: Flat & Hierarchical Web Site Organization

Once you have more than a few pages, a Web site with the structure on the right is easier for readers to find their way around; it will also be easier to reorganize and extend without touching the top level page.

Obviously each page should have links to any related sub-pages. You can also make life easier for your readers if each page provides a link to

- ❏ the top level page (Home Page),
- ❏ the main page of the topic area,
- ❏ other relevant pages on your site.

While using links to provide an overall structure is important, don't forget that you can link from one page to *any* other page. So although you might have a main "document archive" page which provides a link, say, to an individual will transcript, you can also create links to that will transcript from the individual's entry on the family tree pages, or from a narrative about the individual. However, it's important not to overdo this — readers can easily get disorientated if there are too many different ways to move between pages on your site.

Links to other Web pages outside your own site are not necessary, and will always be less important than the information you yourself are supplying. But it's a simple matter to set aside an area on your Home Page, or even a separate page, to provide links to sites with related information: Web sites of other individuals researching the same surnames; local and family history societies for your ancestors' places of origin; resources for particular genealogical subjects relevant to your ancestors (e.g. naval genealogy, Scottish clans). If you want other genealogists to include links to your Web site on their pages, you will need an area for reciprocal links.

It may be tempting to add lots of external links, and a genealogical page allows plenty of scope. But bear in mind that if someone clicks an external link they leave your site, and may not return. External links are best used sparingly, or cordoned off in their own area.

THE LAYOUT

The main layout facilities provided by HTML are as follows:

- ❏ six levels of heading
- ❏ horizontal rules to divide up the page
- ❏ numbered and bulleted lists
- ❏ bold, italic, and other character formatting features
- ❏ font size changes
- ❏ left, right and center justification
- ❏ tables
- ❏ a number of text and image alignment options

Further control of presentation can be achieved by the use of style sheets (see p. 61). Note that some features found in word-processed documents are not available in HTML: tabs, columns, footnotes, and page breaks, for example.

The Look of Your Pages

Although people will be coming to your pages primarily for information, it is obviously preferable to have pages that look good. Initially, when planning your site, you might decide it's better to make information available immediately, and then devote time to improving the look of the pages later — a good-looking page with no useful information is a waste of time for genealogical purposes; a dull-looking page with interesting content will still be worth visiting. The following sections look at the techniques that are available to make your pages visually interesting (or at least not dull).

USING GRAPHICS

An obvious way to add visual interest to your pages is to add some graphics. There are three distinct ways of using graphics on Web pages:

- ❏ **Illustrations:** images that are there for their pictorial content — a photograph of an ancestor, a map of a village, a scanned image of an original document.
- ❏ **Icons:** images whose sole function is graphical — to highlight certain points on the page, to provide navigational assistance, or just to add visual variety to the page.[25]

---

[25] Although they differ in function, what I have here called *illustrations* and *icons* are a single type of feature (usually called **in-line graphics**) from the point of view of how they are created. See the next chapter.

❏ **Background Images:** images that form a repeating "tiled" background to the whole page.

Before you fill your pages with graphics, however, you need to bear in mind three problems they bring:

❏ they slow down the retrieval of the page for the reader;
❏ illustrations can use up relatively large amounts of your Web space;
❏ too many graphics can make a page look muddled.

If you have a reasonable amount of Web space and illustrations are essential, then one solution to the first problem is to have small versions of images (often called **thumbnails**), which can be clicked on to load a larger, higher resolution version of the same image. This means that only those readers who are interested in the full image need download it.[26]

However, while illustrations may take up a lot of space and increase downloading time, a set of icons that can be used to highlight certain information or provide navigational help for your readers will be well worth the small amount of space they take (quite apart from helping to give your pages a consistent design). This is because each icon only needs to be stored once, no matter how often it is used on your pages, and downloaded once in any visit to your site. The look of pages can be significantly improved by using, for example, colored bullets for lists, or an icon to take people back to your Home Page. While you will probably have to create your own illustrations, by scanning photographs and documents, there are thousands of icons available on the Web which you can borrow for your own pages.§[27] You can also save a copy of any image you find on another Web page (see your browser documentation if you do not know how to do this), though of course you may need permission from the copyright owner before using it. If you want to create your own icons, you'll need some sort of graphics package.

Another way of providing graphical variety is to use a background image for your pages. The background image is "tiled" to form a repeating backdrop to the whole page, but you only need one copy of the file. Also, if you use the same image on all your pages, the browser will only need to download the image from the server for the first page. A popular use for backgrounds is to have not a picture, but a texture providing a seamless backdrop to the whole page. Background images have the disadvantage of increasing the download time of your page, and, if chosen carelessly, may make text difficult to read. But a well-chosen background can help to make your pages distinctive and visually more interesting. Again, there are plenty of background textures available for downloading; or, with suitable software and graphics skills, you can create your own.§

---

[26] See, for example, the thumbnails of certificates at *http://www.oz.net/~markhow/ukbirths.htm*, which link to full size images. The thumbnails are about a tenth of the size of the full images.

[27] While it's important to respect copyright on the Web, as elsewhere, it is a fair assumption that someone publishing a collection of icons or colored bullets on a Web page intends, in the absence of any statement to the contrary, to make them freely available.

IMAGE FORMATS

There are two main image formats used on the Web: GIF and JPEG. Images in any other format will need to be converted to GIF or JPEG if your readers are to see them on screen; otherwise they will only be able to download them. Any graphics editor should be able to carry out conversion to these formats.§ A further format called PNG has been designed specifically for the Web, but is not yet widely used.

Both GIF and JPEG formats use compression to make files smaller than they would otherwise be, but the two formats have different strengths and weaknesses. GIFs can have only a limited number of colors (up to 256), but the advantage is that the fewer colors they have, and the more blocks of identical color, the smaller the file. Conversely, the more different colors and the more subtle the color variation, the larger the GIF file. This makes the GIF format ideal for icons, line drawings and the like, but less suitable for photographic images. An important advantage of the GIF format is that it uses "loss-less" compression, that is, the compression process does not destroy any information and the image will not lose any of its original color or detail. But 256 colors is not enough to show the subtle skin-tones in a color portrait, and the "dithering" effect which comes from not having enough colors available can be seen in the rightmost image in Fig. 10.

JPEG images can contain up to 16 million colors (but bear in mind that not all computer displays can show all of these) and can be created with different amounts of compression. However, the more the image file is compressed, the more image quality is compromised — this is called "lossy" compression — and the JPEG format really only makes sense for photographs or graphic images where subtlety of color and shading are important. The amount of compression used for an individual JPEG image can be chosen to achieve the best compromise between file size and image quality.

USING COLOR

Even without using images, you can give your pages a bit more interest by use of color. HTML allows you to specify

- ❏ a background color for the whole page,
- ❏ text color (from an individual letter, to the whole page),
- ❏ the colors for links,
- ❏ background colors for individual table cells.

With WYSIWYG software you'll probably be able to select colors from a color palette.

Theoretically, you have up to 16 million colors to play with, but there are very good technical reasons for using a more restricted palette, except in high-quality images. In order to display 16 million colors, a computer needs a graphics card with at least 4MB of memory. A computer with less will only be able to show 256 colors, and any color that is not one of these 256 will be approximated by "dithering," that is, mixing pixels of two similar colors, the effect of which is not particularly appealing. Outside the realms of photography or art, there is no real justification for worrying about that degree of color accuracy anyway — readers will have a range of different computers, graphics cards, monitors and graphics configurations which will defy any attempt at

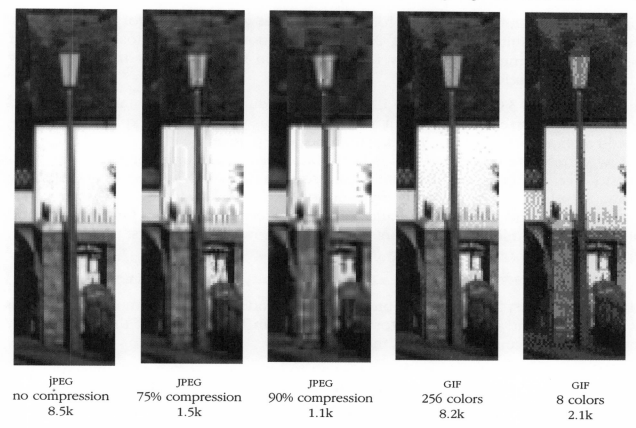

jPEG	JPEG	JPEG	GIF	GIF
no compression	75% compression	90% compression	256 colors	8 colors
8.5k	1.5k	1.1k	8.2k	2.1k

The image shows a lamp-post outside Pevensey Court House, scanned from a photograph. The original size of the images is 47 x 166 pixels and they are shown here enlarged about 4 times. Note how the straight lines of the lamp-post are distorted or blurred as the image becomes smaller, and quality is compromised. A Windows bitmap of the same image is 23k in size.

Fig. 10: Image Formats

the sort of color matching one expects of professional color printing. Instead, it's best to restrict oneself to what is called the "browser-safe palette" of 216 colors which are guaranteed to display more or less accurately, without dithering, on any color system.[28] Even so, be wary of using color to convey information (say, putting all names of male ancestors in blue) because (a) readers with text-only browsers will not see the colors, and (b) some readers will have their browser configured to ignore color specifications contained in a page.

USING FONTS

The relation between fonts and the Web is currently in a state of transition. The original design of HTML did not have any way of allowing the use of specific fonts on a Web page. Browsers could, and still do, choose between a proportional font and

---

[28] If your computer display is set for 256 colors or fewer, you can see the dithering effect at *http:// www.walrus.dircon.co.uk/wpg/unsafe.html*, and the browser-safe palette at *http://www.walrus.dircon.co.uk/wpg/ safe.html*.

a fixed width font, the latter used for displaying text with a number of particular tags. These fonts default to Times and Courier on Windows and Macintosh systems, but the user can change these to any font installed on his or her system, just like any other browser preferences.

Then, with HTML 3.0, Netscape and Microsoft introduced a **<FONT>** tag, mainly used to control font size and color, but which in Microsoft's Internet Explorer also supported a choice of font face. This tag then became part of the HTML 3.2 standard, and is now widely used. The problem is that a browser can use only fonts that are available to it on the machine it is running on, something a Web author cannot possibly know. So while you can specify any font you like when designing a Web page, the chances of it appearing on the reader's browser are unpredictable. One way around this is to specify a list of similar fonts and let the browser use the first one it can find. So, for example, on encountering the tag:

<FONT FACE="Arial, Helvetica, sans-serif">

a browser will first look for Arial (present on all Windows systems), then for Helvetica (which it will find on any Macintosh), and if it can find neither of those it will use any sans-serif face it can find on the system.

The other way is to use a graphics program to turn the text in a particular font into a graphic. Obviously this is not something you would want to do for an entire page, but it's a very useful way of getting a precise font match on something like a logo, where it might be important not to have some unspecified, vaguely similar font.

A further, though only partial, solution is to use Microsoft's Web fonts. These are fonts that have been designed specifically for viewing on screen and have good readability. They are included in Internet Explorer on both Mac and Windows platforms. If you do not use Explorer, they are freely downloadable from Microsoft's Web site.[29] Of course, you cannot rely on all readers having these fonts installed, but many will.

In the future, we will see facilities for a font that is required on a page to be loaded with that page, in the same way that graphics are now. Software companies and W3C are working towards this currently, though there are still technical and copyright problems to be solved.[30]

Arial Black	**ABCabc**
Comic Sans	ABCabc
Georgia	ABCabc
Impact	**ABCabc**
Trebuchet	ABCabc
Verdana	ABCabc
[Webdings]	🏙✔🚲

Fig. 11: Microsoft's Typefaces for the Web

---

[29] *http://www.microsoft.com/truetype/fontpack/win.htm.*

[30] Microsoft already has what it calls a "Web Embedding Fonts Tool," but this only works with Internet Explorer. See *http://www.microsoft.com/typography/web/embedding/default.htm.*

Good and Bad Web Design

Even if you've never designed anything before, you will have been exposed to information in printed form which draws upon over 1,000 years of tradition and experience in how to present information on the physical page of a book, so understanding what makes a word-processed document look good is not particularly taxing. On the other hand, no one has more than 6 years of experience in designing Web pages, or more than 20 years in designing hypertext systems. This means that the art of Web design is still in its infancy. Nonetheless, it's clear that there are really two components to it:

- ❏ the individual pages should be well designed — they should be visually clear and information should be easy to read;
- ❏ the site as a whole should be well designed — it should be easy to see what's on the site and how to find one's way around.

The important question to keep in mind is: whom is your site aimed at? Since the purpose of a genealogical site must be to provide information, any purely graphical elements should serve that information and should not be dominant. Also, remember that most readers will be coming to your site over a phone line and a modem rather than via a fast permanent connection, so you shouldn't have anything on your pages that causes them to download more slowly than they need to. Experience shows that people simply don't wait for pages that are slow to download — at least, not unless they are sure that the information will be of interest.

Most books on Web publishing will offer some guidance on design issues. Of the material freely available on the Web, the Yale Web Style Guide is highly recommended, while "Web Pages That Suck" will show you some of the things to avoid.[31]

Some of the basic things to avoid in page design are

- ❏ Excessive use of bold or upper case,
- ❏ Excessive use of headings or large font sizes,
- ❏ Backgrounds or color combinations that make the text hard to read,
- ❏ Using a different background or color scheme on every page,
- ❏ Lots of unnecessary graphics,
- ❏ Adding a feature just because you know how to do it and want to try it out.

In both page and site design, the best advice is to keep it simple and keep it clear. It *is* possible to pack a lot of information on a Web page and have complex graphic design, but a glance at a few corporate Web sites should convince you that even professional designers find it hard to do this well.

Legal and Ethical Issues

COPYRIGHT

It is important to bear in mind that Web publishing is subject to the same copyright restrictions as any other form of publishing: if you take material from a copyright

---

[31] *http://info.med.yale.edu/caim/manual/contents.html* and *http://www.webpagesthatsuck.com/*, respectively.

source without permission, you are likely to be breaking copyright legislation.[32] Since, as an individual family historian, you're not gaining any financial advantage from the material, and are probably not causing financial loss to the copyright owner, you may well feel that it's very unfair that you should not be able to do so. But putting something on the Web is publishing it, and you are not entitled to publish others' intellectual property without their permission on the Web any more than you would be on paper. You should always ask for permission to reproduce text if you are in any doubt about its copyright status. The same applies to logos, photographs, or other scanned images. Obviously, putting your family photographs on the Web is not a problem, but you are not going to be able to scan photographs from a recent book for your Web site without permission. Recent legislation[33] also protects the compilers of databases from "unfair extraction" — you can't simply extract material on your surname from a CD-ROM or the IGI and put it on your Web site without permission, though, of course, the facts that you have derived from these sources are not themselves protected by copyright.

You should also bear in mind that placing your own material on the Web could lead to others infringing your copyright. Of course this can happen with a book, too, but it's much easier with digital material. There are two distinct dangers. There are a few people who will unscrupulously republish or distribute your copyright material without permission, sometimes even for profit. Secondly, not all users of the Internet are actually aware of current copyright law (which in the U.S., for example, has recently changed) and therefore copy material illegally though without any dishonest intent. This means that you should be very cautious about putting your own material on the Web if you are in any way concerned about the use to which it may be put by others. If you have a substantial database, for example, it may be better to place just an index to it on-line, or provide access only via a search facility (see p. 63). This is particularly the case if you are a professional genealogist or a family history society and derive income from your data collections. On the other hand there's no point in being too cautious — if your site is devoid of information, there's no point in creating it, as no one will want to look at it anyway.

PRIVACY

Unlike the situation with copyright, there is no international treaty that sets out the circumstances in which it is or is not permissible to publish personal information about private individuals, though the European Union, for example, has its own very stringent laws in this area. But regardless of the legal situation, it is obviously a discourtesy to publish personal information about living persons without their permission, and this is something that is universally agreed upon among genealogists. This means that if you are going to turn your GEDCOM file into a set of Web pages, or

---

[32] The US Copyright Office has a *Copyright Basics* circular on the Web at *http://www.loc.gov/copyright/circs/index.html#circ1*. Many of the copyright issues relating to the Web are discussed in the *Web Law FAQ* at *http://www.patents.com/weblaw.sht*.

[33] The 1996 WIPO COPYRIGHT TREATY, text on-line at *http://www.wipo.org/eng/diplconf/distrib/94dc.htm*

make it available for downloading, you should take care to exclude living individuals, unless you have their agreement. Probably for your immediate family, this is not a big issue, but you should think carefully if you are going to produce pages listing, say, all known descendants of some ancestor. Remember that some of your relatives, particularly the older ones, may be extremely sensitive about family information, even about relatives no longer alive, and may not be happy to see it published.[34]

There are several ways of ensuring that information about living persons is not published on your Web site:

- ❑ a genealogy package with Web facilities should permit you to exclude living persons from your GEDCOM file (usually by selecting a subset of individuals to export);
- ❑ many of the GEDCOM converters have "privacy" facilities (see p. 31);
- ❑ there are a number of utilities specifically designed to remove living persons from a GEDCOM file before conversion.

The following programs have facilities for removing sensitive information from a GEDCOM file:

GEDClean	*http://www.raynorshyn.com/gedclean/*
GEDLiving	*http://www.rootsweb.com/~gumby/ged.html*
GEDPrivy	*http://hometown.aol.com/gedprivy/index.html*
GEDStrip	*http://webhome.idirect.com/~naylor/gedstrip.htm*
Res Privata	*http://www.ozemail.com.au/~naibor/rpriv.html*

---

[34] See also Myra Vanderpool Gormley, "Exposing Our Families to the Internet" at *http://www.ancestry.com/home/ Myra_Vanderpool_Gormley/Shaking_Family_Tree06-19-97.htm* and Norris M. Taylor, Jr., "Privacy on the Internet. Effect on Genealogy" at *http://members.aol.com/jacob59/more/otherstuff/priv.html*.

5. Creating the Pages

This chapter will look at the basics of creating a simple Web page using a text editor. You could also use a word-processor, as long as you remember to use your word-processor's *save as text* or *save as ASCII* option to save the file — do *not* save your page in your normal word-processor format, as your browser will not be able to make any sense of it.

The purpose of this section is not to teach you all there is to know about Web page creation, and it is not structured as a tutorial, but it will give you an idea of what sort of page layout and design facilities are available, and how to make use of them. (The information in this chapter is fairly detailed and you may want to skip it if you're not ready to try creating pages at this stage.)

A Skeleton Page

Regardless of the content of a Web page, there are certain basic minimum requirements:

- ❏ the page must start with an **<HTML>** tag, and end with an **</HTML>** tag;
- ❏ the page must have a pair of **<HEAD>…</HEAD>** and **<BODY>…</BODY>** tags to mark out the two main components of the page (and they must be in that order, head before body);
- ❏ inside the **<HEAD>** area, there must be a pair of **<TITLE>…</TITLE>** tags;
- ❏ the entire visible content of your page must go in the **<BODY>** section; the **<HEAD>** is only used for the **<TITLE>** and for other information not displayed on the page.

If you don't observe these requirements you will get unpredictable results. For example, if you type some text in the **<HEAD>** instead of the **<BODY>**, some browsers will ignore it, others will display it on screen.

Here's a basic, minimal page:

```
<HTML>
   <HEAD>
      <TITLE>This where the page title goes</TITLE>
   </HEAD>
   <BODY>
      This is where the contents of your page go
   </BODY>
</HTML>
```

I've used indentation and made the tags bold here simply to make the structure more obvious. Since *all* page design is done with tags, any line breaks, tabs, indents, extra spaces, etc., that you add do not have any effect on the final appearance of the page. The following example will produce *exactly the same* page as the previous one:

```
<HTML> <HEAD> <TITLE> This is

where the page title goes</TITLE> </HEAD> <BODY>This is where
the contents of your page go </BODY> </HTML>
```

To Create a Basic Page

1. Start your text editor.[35]

2. Type in the text as it is in the first example above (ignore the indentation).

3. Save the text with a filename such as *test.html* (or *test.htm* in DOS or Windows 3.1).[36]

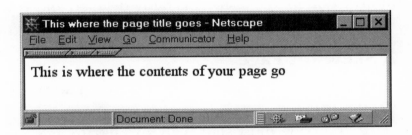

**Fig. 12: The Skeleton Page
Viewed in Netscape**

4. To view the page: start your browser and open the file (in Netscape and Explorer this option is on the **File** menu; for other browsers see the on-line help if you do not know how to load a file from disk).

Understanding Tags

Before you start trying out any of the material in the following sections, there are five key things about HTML tags that you need to know:

1. *All* page formatting is achieved by using tags. Browsers will *ignore* any formatting that is not indicated by tags, in particular, tabs, line breaks, multiple spaces. Tabs and multiple spaces are not available in HTML. Line breaks are created by special line break tags.

2. All HTML tags consist of angled brackets containing the tag **identifier**, e.g. **<HR>**, the tag that indicates a horizontal rule.

---

[35] Windows users will find the text editor Notepad via Start menu | Programs | Accessories. Mac users can use Claris Works/Appleworks and remember to save files as Text (via the Save As option on the File menu), or use BBEdit Lite, which can be downloaded free of charge from *http://www.barebones.com/free/bbedit_lite.html*.

[36] You should always use either *.html* or *.htm* as the filename extension for Web pages, so that browsers can recognize them as such. On systems which do not allow extensions longer than 3 letters (such as DOS or Windows 3.1) you will need to use the latter.

3. Some tags are single, others come in pairs. Paired tags (consisting of a start tag and an end tag) enclose the material to which they apply, e.g. **<B>** is the start tag for a section of bold text, **</B>** is the end tag, and everything between them will be in bold. End tags always have **/** before the tag identifier.

4. You cannot invent your own tags; you can only use those which are already defined.

5. Tags are not case sensitive: **<HR>** and **<hr>**, or even **<hR>**, will all produce a horizontal rule. (However, tags are often typed in upper case, as this makes it easy for a human reader to spot the tags when reading the HTML source for a page.)

If you try out the material in this chapter and it doesn't seem to come out right, experience suggests that in almost every case it will be because you have made a typing error, and not because there's something wrong with your browser. Check the tags carefully, especially the spelling — browsers cannot cope with misspelled or missing tags. Check that you have matching start and end tags where required.

Basic Page Design

ORGANIZING YOUR PAGE

While you could offer on your Web pages lumps of undifferentiated text, this is not very considerate to your readers: they will find it hard to read, and it will not be easy for them to see quickly what the page contains. HTML provides three general ways of giving the content of your page an obvious structure:

❑ paragraphs
❑ headings
❑ rules

The paragraph tag **<P>** splits text into paragraphs.[37] When a browser comes across this tag it will start a new line, and will also leave an extra blank line before the next paragraph. The browser will automatically word-wrap the text, and it will adapt the line length to the width of the browser window, so that the reader will not miss any text. Long paragraphs can be very hard to read on-screen — 6 to 10 lines at full screen width is probably enough for one paragraph.

There are 6 levels of headings available, with 1 being the most important, 6 the least important. Each heading is indicated by a pair of tags enclosing the text of the heading, and the browser will automatically put each heading on a line by itself, separate from any paragraph text. The tags are **<H1>…</H1>** to **<H6>…</H6>**. These tags are best used in a strictly hierarchical manner, **<H1>** for the main heading at the top of the page, **<H2>** for the first level of sub-heading, etc. A typical beginner's mistake

---

[37] Strictly, paragraphing requires a pair of tags: **<P>** to start a paragraph and **</P>** to end it. However, since **<P>**, and many other tags such as the heading tags, *imply* the end of the preceding paragraph it can be omitted. Some editing software will automatically insert **</P>**, some won't.

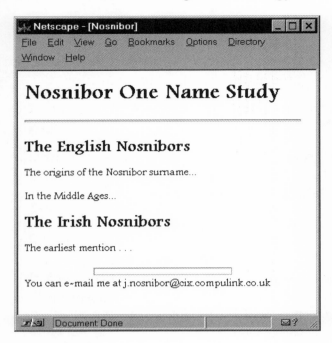

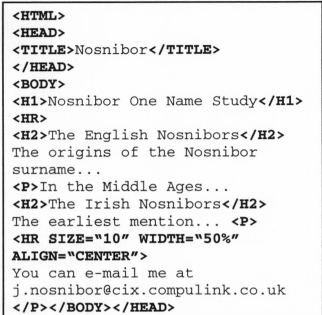

```
<HTML>
<HEAD>
<TITLE>Nosnibor</TITLE>
</HEAD>
<BODY>
<H1>Nosnibor One Name Study</H1>
<HR>
<H2>The English Nosnibors</H2>
The origins of the Nosnibor
surname...
<P>In the Middle Ages...
<H2>The Irish Nosnibors</H2>
The earliest mention... <P>
<HR SIZE="10" WIDTH="50%"
ALIGN="CENTER">
You can e-mail me at
j.nosnibor@cix.compulink.co.uk
</P></BODY></HEAD>
```

Fig. 13: Using Headings and Rules

is to choose whichever level of heading looks best on your browser, forgetting that on another browser, with different user options, it may look significantly larger or smaller. Also, proper use of headings will improve indexing by search engines. Browsers will automatically end a paragraph before a heading and start a new one after, so you do not need to use the **<P>** tag with headings.

It is often useful to break up the text into sections, and HTML provides a Horizontal Rule (the tag is **<HR>**) which can be used for this purpose. You can also specify the thickness of the rule, the width, and the alignment. This is done by inserting additional information (called **attributes**[38]) into the tag after the identifier. You can see an example of this in Fig. 13, but you'll need to consult reference material for full details.§

CHARACTER FORMATTING

There is a range of character formatting facilities in HTML. These always involve using paired tags that surround the text to be formatted. The most commonly used ones are for bold, italic, and a typewriter font (these effects can also be combined):

`This point is <B>important</B>`	this point is **important**
`<I>Computers in Genealogy</I>`	*Computers in Genealogy*
`This is <TT>typescript</TT>`	this is `typescript`
`This is <B><I>very important</I></B>`	this is ***very important***

---

[38] Many other tags can have attributes.

```
Martin Christian had
three children by his
second marriage:
<OL>
<LI>Abraham, bapt. 1602
<LI>Mary, bapt. 1606
<LI>Sarah, bapt. 1611
</OL>
Abraham inherited
<UL>
<LI>A cupboard
<LI>A pewter plate
<LI>One pound
</UL>
```

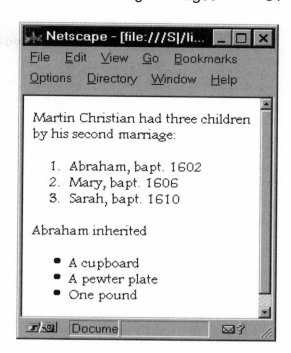

Fig. 14: The Two Main Types of Lists

HTML also allows you to control the font size of any piece of text, though this is easily overdone. More extensive character formatting is available with style sheets (see p. 61).

LINE BREAKS

Line breaks in the text file that makes up a Web page are ignored by the browser, which automatically starts a new line after certain features, such as headings and horizontal rules, but otherwise needs a tag. HTML distinguishes between a paragraph break, which is followed by additional space, and a simple line break, the tag for which is **
**. This is typically used for things like addresses, where you don't want the extra blank lines which you would get with a paragraph break.

LISTS

HTML provides two main types of lists: an **ordered list**, where the items are numbered in sequence, and an **unordered list**, where each item is preceded by a bullet. Lists are created by having a pair of list tags to contain the list (**<OL>...</OL>** for an ordered list, **<UL>...</UL>** for an unordered list), and each item in the list is preceded by the **list item** tag **<LI>**.[39] The browser automatically adds the numbers or bullets, and adds blank lines before and after the list (see Fig. 14). It is also possible to have nested lists, i.e. lists within lists.

---

[39] Like the paragraph tag **<P>**, the list item tag **<LI>** can have an end tag **</LI>**, but as the start of the next list item or the end of the list implies the end of the previous list item, it can be omitted.

IMAGES

As explained in the previous chapter, each graphic image on a Web page is stored as a separate file and is not part of the page as such. The text of the page simply contains a special tag **<IMG>** which indicates to the browser the name of the image file. For example, the tag **<IMG SRC="map.gif">** tells the browser to load an image, and that the filename of the image (**SRC** is short for "source") is *map.gif*. HTML also provides various options for the relative alignment of text and images.

An important consideration when using images is to provide for those readers using text-only browsers or who have image loading turned off. There is a special attribute for the **<IMG>** tag which allows you to specify some text to be displayed for any image that is not shown on the page. The tag

<IMG SRC="gr.jpg" ALT="My grandmother at the age of 6">

would display the text after **ALT** whenever the image doesn't appear. In some browsers this text will also appear when you move the mouse over it and so serves as a caption.

CREATING LINKS

Obviously each Web page on your site is not isolated. At the very least you will have a main page with links to your other pages. But you may well have links to pages on other Web sites. It is also possible to have links that take you to a point on the same page.

Links are created by the use of a pair of Anchor tags **<A>...</A>**, which surround the text that is to function as the hot spot and the URL of the page the browser is to fetch when the hot spot is selected or clicked on with the mouse. The general format is

<A HREF="*the-URL-of-the-relevant-page***">text of hot spot</A>**

e.g.,   **<A HREF="**http://www.walrus.dircon.co.uk/wpg/**">This book</A>**

On a browser the text of the hot spot will normally appear in blue and be underlined. The URL of the page linked to will not appear on the page itself, though it will be displayed in the status bar at the bottom of the browser window when the reader moves the mouse over the hot spot. **HREF**, incidentally, is short for "hypertext reference."

You can also use an image as a hot spot: put the appropriate image tag **<IMG SRC="...">** instead of the hot spot text, and then clicking on the image will take you to the linked page.

For pages that reside on a different server from the page itself, you must give the full URL — the **absolute** URL, as it's called — containing the name of the server and the **pathname** for the correct page (see p. 14). If, however, you are linking to a page on the same server, you can give what's called a **relative** reference, i.e. the address of the page relative to the page you will be coming from. For example, supposing you have a page whose address is

http://www.walrus.dircon.co.uk/wpg/software.html

and you want to create a link to

http://www.walrus.dircon.co.uk/wpg/reference.html

you could indicate this simply with the tags **<A HREF="reference.html">...</A>**. If you just give a file name, the browser will assume the file is on the same server and in the same directory as the current page. For this reason, if you keep all your pages in one directory, you can make links between them simply by giving the filename and not the complete URL. Of course, you may be using several different directories/folders for your files, in which case you will have to give the directory name as well as the file name. For example, on the Web site for this book, all the figures (all those that are not just screenshots of existing Web pages) are held in a separate directory called *figures*, so links to the figures from the main page require tags such as **<A HREF="figures/fig9.html">...</A>**, or whatever.

An important technique for making your pages easy to navigate, particularly for longer pages, is to have, near the top of the page, a set of links to the various sections of the page itself, as in Fig. 15, which shows one of the *Computers in Genealogy* pages. Clicking on any of the underlined words under the heading takes you not to another Web page but down to the start of the relevant section on the same page.

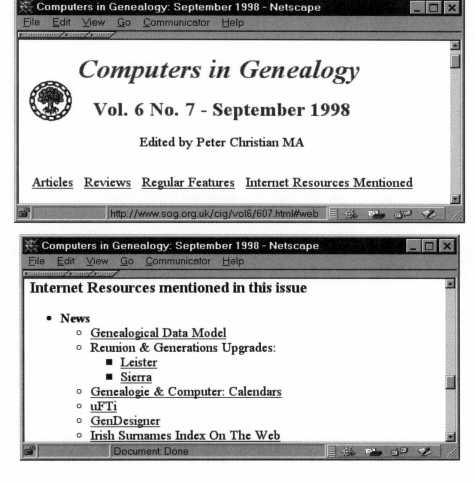

Fig. 15: Navigation Aids *within* a Page

You need two separate pairs of tags on the page to achieve this. First you select the point at which you want to end up (often called the **target**), and you put a special form of the **<A>** tag there to *name* it. You can now have an **<A>** tag elsewhere on this page, which, instead of a URL, contains a hypertext reference to this name. (In this reference, the name is preceded by the # character so that the browser can tell that it's a page location and not a filename.) So at the top of this *CiG* page is the hot spot and the linking information, for example:

<A HREF="#web">Internet resources mentioned**</A>**

When the browser sees **#web**, it will look through the page to try and find a location (**<A NAME=...>**) named **web**, and will come across:

<A NAME="web"><H3>Internet resources mentioned in this issue**</H3></A>**

and automatically scroll down to that point in the page. In this way, you can give your page a list of contents, and the reader can immediately see what the page contains and can easily get to the section of interest.[40] This is a good way of making a long page easier to use.

Another very useful type of link is an e-mail link: when the reader clicks on the hot spot, the browser will bring up an e-mail window with the correct e-mail address already filled in, and you can simply type a message and send it (assuming you have configured your browser's e-mail facility). This is done by having a "mailto" URL, something like:

<A HREF="mailto:cig@sog.org.uk">The Editor</A>

which would allow you to e-mail the editor of *CiG* by clicking on the words *The Editor*.

TABLES

You might think that the only use for tables is to present tabular information such as the database extract in Fig. 2 (p. 20), or the parish register search results in Fig. 17 (p. 63), but in HTML tables are an extremely flexible layout tool for positioning text and graphics on the page, since they allow you to split a page into regions and control their position and size (see Fig. 16). You can put either text or images into any cell in a table, which makes it a relatively good way to align a group of images and text paragraphs, even when the images are different sizes and the text different lengths. For tabular data, tables can be given borders, while for layout they are usually left without.[41]

---

[40] You can in fact use these name references in combination with a full URL. For example, you could refer to the Internet resources section of this page as *http://www.sog.org.uk/cig/vol6/607.html#web* from anywhere on the Internet (try this in your browser). Of course, you can only do this if the author of the page has included named locations in the page.

[41] A very elaborate use of tables can be seen on the UK Public Record Office Home Page (*http://www.pro.gov.uk/*), where some of the individual cells contain further tables.

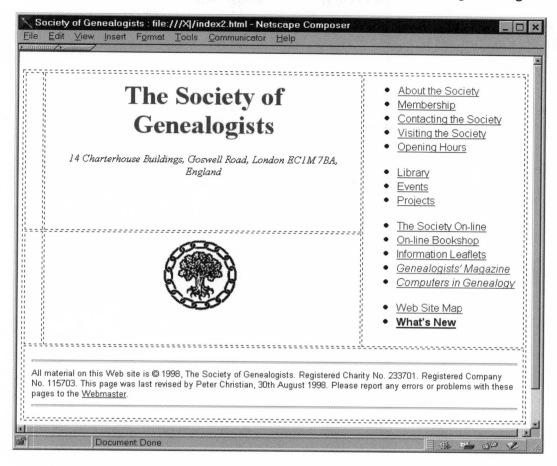

Fig. 16: Using Tables for Layout

The Society of Genealogists Home Page (*http://www.sog.org.uk/*) uses a table to split the page into a number of boxes for the positioning of the separate components of the page. This screenshot is from Netscape Composer, with double dotted lines showing the boundaries of the table cells. Since the table has no border, these lines do not show up in the browser window.

SPECIAL CHARACTERS

One of the problems in any sort of textual work on computers is that different types of computers and different operating systems use different character sets. If HTML is designed to work on *any* computer, how does it get around this problem? It does so by restricting its basic character set to numbers, letters, and a few punctuation marks, and having a special way of indicating all other characters. Each character (including all the normal ones) has a number, and the character can be entered into a Web page by typing the number between an ampersand and a semi-colon. For example the copyright symbol © is represented as **©** and the "less than" sign < (which starts all tags, and so can't be used as a text character in its own right) is **<**. But because this is not easy to remember, many frequently used special characters can also be referred to by a memorable name or abbreviation, **©** and **<** being used for © and <. This also includes foreign characters such as é (**é** or **é**) or ö (**ö** or **ö**). The ampersand itself is **&** or **&**.

If you are using an HTML-aware word-processor or a Web authoring package you will not need to worry about this, as the software should take care of it automatically. Many HTML editors provide easy ways of entering these characters. Otherwise you will need to look them up.§

6. Going Public

Publishing Your Pages

Once you have finished creating your pages and you have thoroughly tested and spell-checked them, you make them public by uploading them to the Web server belonging to your Internet provider. The exact process by which you do this will depend on how your provider organizes Web space on their system. You should make sure you have two pieces of information from your provider:

❑ how to access your Web space on their system to upload the pages, and
❑ the URL of your Home Page once it is mounted on their system.

The normal method of copying files to a server of any sort is to use a program called FTP. If you have already used this to download software from software archives, you will be familiar with the general process, and it works in the same way if you want to upload files. However, because you will be uploading to your own private area you will need to use your own login and password.

Some Web authoring tools come with built-in utilities to upload your pages. For example, CompuServe's Home Page Wizard is accompanied by the Home Page Publishing Wizard, which automates the process of uploading your pages. A more general tool is Microsoft's Web Publishing Wizard,[42] while Netscape Composer provides what it calls "one button publishing," both of which automate uploading your pages. Some other HTML tools have similar utilities.

The URL of your pages will depend on what sort of Internet account you have. For many ISPs it will simply be the name of the provider's server followed by your own identifier. For my own genealogy pages it is *http://homepages.gold.ac.uk/peter/*, i.e. the URL of the Web server on which my pages are located, followed by my username on that system. On CompuServe it would be *http://ourworld.compuserve.com/ homepages/user-id/* with your CompuServe user-id as the last element. Some ISPs, however, provide subscribers with their own **domain name**, so that it appears that each user has his own personal Web server, rather than simply having his own directory on a general server (this is called a **virtual server**). For example, the Web pages for this book are on *http://www.walrus.dircon.co.uk/*, which are in reality just located in my own directory on *http://www.dircon.co.uk/* where *walrus* is my username.

Your ISP should provide documentation about what you need to do (including how to use FTP to upload pages) and provide support.

---

[42] Free, from *http://www.microsoft.com/windows/software/webpost/*

Getting Readers for Your Pages

Once your pages are mounted on the server, you will want to publicize them. This not only makes sure people have a better chance of finding out about your pages, but also is a useful way to get people with different browsers to make sure your pages look all right, and spot any errors you have missed. The following sections look at the main ways of making your pages known.

MAILING LISTS & NEWSGROUPS

Genealogy mailing lists and newsgroups are good places to announce a new genealogical Web site.[43] If you use an on-line service, it will probably also have a suitable place for such announcements, for example the genealogy forums on CompuServe. Remember to give the full URL of your page and a brief description of what's there. Mention the main surnames covered, any particular geographical areas for which you have material, and any transcripts of original source material. You can also use newsgroups and mailing lists to announce any major changes to your site, especially if you add any new source materials. But don't overdo it — the whole world doesn't want to know each time you correct a spelling mistake on one of your pages! Bear in mind that you will generally only be able to post this information in mailing lists you subscribe to, and be careful to post only where it's relevant. Dick Eastman's weekly newsletter regularly mentions new genealogical Web pages under the heading "Home Pages Highlighted."[44]

General places for posting information about new genealogical Web sites are the NEW-GEN-URL mailing list and the GENCMP-L mailing list.[45] The latter is gatewayed with the newsgroup **soc.genealogy.computing** to which you can post without subscribing to the mailing list. There are also many regional, local, and ethnic mailing lists, where your posting will be seen by readers who share some of your genealogical background.

RECIPROCAL LINKS

Many genealogists are happy to add links to other genealogy pages. Whenever you come across another genealogy page offering this facility, make use of it, especially if it deals with interests similar to your own. But if you do this, you should expect to return the favor, and should have an area set aside on your pages for these reciprocal links. The largest collection of links to personal genealogy pages is probably the one on Cyndi's List.[46]

GENDEX

Several of the GEDCOM converters automatically create a file called *gendex.txt*, which lists all the individuals in the file with birth and death details. Once you have up-

---

[43] If you don't know how to use mailing lists or newsgroups, look at any of the Internet genealogy books.

[44] An index to back issues can be found at *http://www.ancestry.com/columns/eastman/index.htm*.

[45] See *http://www.rootsweb.com/~maillist/misc/index.html*.

[46] *http://www.CyndisList.com/personal.htm*

loaded your Web pages to the server (including *gendex.txt*), you can submit details to Gene Stark's GENDEX site,[47] which will then add the details from your *gendex.txt* to a central searchable index with links to your site. The table on p. 31 indicates which converters support GENDEX.

SEARCH ENGINES

The best way to ensure that people can find your page is to submit the details to one or more of the **search engines** on the Web. On the home page of each one, there should be a link taking you to a page where you can submit details. You only need to submit the details of your main genealogy page, as most search engines will come and explore your Web site for themselves, once they know of its existence. You should make sure you register your Web site with AltaVista,[48] which is probably the most widely used search engine, and if possible with some of the others. Of course, submitting details of your page to a lot of different search engines is a chore, so there are some special Web sites which allow you to submit your URL to a whole range of search engines at once. The best known of these is Submit It, which has a free submission service covering the most widely used search engines.[49]

One important issue is how to ensure that the content of your pages can be accurately indexed and retrieved by a search engine. While some search engines will index much of the text of your pages, there are certain important places on your page that search tools will make particular use of:

- ❏ the page title
- ❏ headings
- ❏ the first paragraphs of text

There is also a special tag you can use in the document **<HEAD>** to summarize the content, the **<META>** tag. The **<META>** tag (for "meta-information") is a general-purpose tag used to provide information *about* the page but which is not actually to be displayed to the reader. The format used to indicate content is:

```
<META NAME="KEYWORDS" CONTENT="genealogy, family history,
Savannah, Georgia, King, Young">
```

You can put any text you like between the quotation marks after **CONTENT**. Many search engines will include the first few lines of text on your page as a description, but you can again use the **<META>** tag to provide a custom description, e.g.

```
<META NAME="Description" CONTENT="The King and Young families
of Savannah, Georgia (1820-present)">
```

There are a number of Web sites that offer advice on ensuring search engines index and retrieve your site effectively.§

---

[47] *http://www.gendex.com/*

[48] *http://www.altavista.com/*

[49] *http://siteowner.linkexchange.com/Free.cfm*. Other examples are Siteowner (*http://www.siteowner.com/*) and !Register It! (*http://www.register-it.com/*).

Maintaining & Improving Your Web Site

One of the main distinctions between Web genealogy and printed genealogy is that once you have your Web site up and running, you can continue to modify it. At the very least, your Web site will need "maintenance," and you will need to do the following:

- ❏ Correct any errors which are brought to your attention.
- ❏ Repair any technical problems, e.g. missing files, links not working.
- ❏ Check periodically that external links are still correct.
- ❏ If you're providing information on behalf of a society, check regularly that the information is current, and remove out-of-date information (or at least flag it as out-of-date).

But you will probably also want to think about improving and expanding it:

- ❏ Consider expanding the content and improving the design (you won't remain satisfied with your first attempts at Web design anyway!).
- ❏ You might want to add further links to sites of related interest.
- ❏ Look at other Web pages for ideas to borrow.
- ❏ Take note of any feedback from readers, particularly if something has been hard to find or use.

7. Advanced Web Facilities

The purpose of this chapter is to look at some of the other features you will find on Web pages, and discuss what is involved in creating them. Unlike the material in previous chapters, these all require some degree of expertise, and are not for beginners. Also, where these facilities depend on the server, Internet providers often make them available only on business accounts. Because these are more complex facilities, this section will not show you how to create them — you will need to refer to reference materials to find out in more detail what is involved, and you may need to invest considerable time in learning how to implement them, or to purchase specialist software tools.

However, one thing to bear in mind is the rapid development of the Web, both in what is technically available and in what is supported by ISPs. Some of the facilities discussed here are currently not practicable for the individual user, but may well be more widely available in the near future. For some of those which at present require considerable expertise, there may be ready-made solutions or easy-to-use tools.

Style Sheets

One of the fundamental conflicts in the development of the Web has been between those concerned with the organization of information and those concerned with graphic design — the Web was designed for scientific communication but is now more used for advertising and selling. Initially, it was the main browser manufacturers, Netscape and Microsoft, who introduced tags to meet the demands of designers. These tags initially only worked with one browser, but many of them were then incorporated into the HTML standard. This means that HTML has become an awkward mixture of features that provide for structured information on the one hand (e.g., heading tags that have a strict hierarchy but no font or color information) and tags whose sole function is to control the *appearance* of the page (e.g., the **<FONT>** tag) on the other. An attempt has now been made to resolve this conflict with a mechanism called **cascading style sheets**, which separates, as far as possible, presentation and information,.

The idea of a style sheet is to have a file that contains all the information about presentation and is linked to any pages that want to use this style. This means that if you wanted to have all the main headings on your site in a blue italic sans-serif font, for example, then instead of having to add this information to every single heading as follows:

```
<H1><I><FONT COLOR="blue" FACE="sans-serif">... </FONT></I></H1>
```

you could simply have a style sheet that says

```
H1 {color: blue; font-family: sans-serif; font-style: italic}
```

and which can be applied to any page you choose. And if you want to switch from blue to red, you only need to edit the style sheet, not every **<FONT>** tag on every page. You can also specify other presentation information that cannot be achieved by HTML tags, such as setting precise margin widths and boxes around text.[50]

In the long term this is clearly the way the Web will develop, but even the latest browsers do not display style sheet-based pages identically, or 100% correctly, for that matter. At present there is little Web authoring software that provides style sheet facilities, but there is plenty of reference material about style sheets on the Web, and they are not difficult to create using an editor.

Image Maps

An **image map** is a special type of graphic image on a Web page. When you click on it with the mouse, exactly which page it links to depends on *where* on the map you click. It need not actually be a map in the cartographic sense, but this is one obvious use that genealogists will find for it. The graphical "button bars" found on many Web sites are often image maps.[51]

Although there are two ways to implement image maps, only one of these is a realistic proposition for the individual user, the **client-side image map**, so called because the map information is stored in the Web page itself (rather than in a separate file on the server). The easiest way to add an image map to a page is to use a special image map utility, which will help you to specify the various regions of the image and will create the tags to be added to the page.§ Some graphics software, too, can handle image maps. You should remember that some readers, accessing your page with text-only browsers or with images switched off, will not be able to see or use image maps, and you will need to provide an alternative for these visitors.

Dynamic Web Pages

One of the major differences between a Web site and a printed book is that the Web supports interaction with the reader. This ranges from trivial effects, e.g. an icon which changes color when you move the mouse over it, to substantial tools, such as a search facility. However, almost all forms of interactivity require some sort of programming, or at least knowledge of how to interface with an existing program. There are three main ways of providing interactivity on a Web page: with forms and CGI scripts, JavaScript, and Java.

FORMS AND CGI SCRIPTS

You will often encounter forms on Web sites. They are useful as a way of collecting input from readers, and are also the way in which readers enter the details of what they want to search for. The completed form sends the information to a program on the Web server called a **CGI script**, usually written in a computer language called PERL, which deals with the data entered in the form and sends a response to the reader.

---

[50] For an example, look at *http://www.sog.org.uk/events/calendar.html* — this page will look different if you save it to a disk and view your saved copy (when it won't find the style sheet).

[51] A good example of an actual map used in this way is the Map of Irish Web Servers at *http://slarti.ucd.ie/maps/ireland.html* or the plan of Christ Church, Oxford, at *http://www.chch.ox.ac.uk/chch/map/chchmap.html*.

In the example shown in Fig. 17, you can use the form to select exactly which records from a database you want to see and then click the Begin Search button. This sends the form data to the server, which then runs a script to look through the database, select the matching records, and present them as a Web page. The virtue for anyone wanting to put transcripts or indexes on-line is that no one can access the whole database at once (and therefore have a complete copy of it) but anyone can extract the information they want.

Designing a Web page with a form is not itself particularly difficult, but for the CGI script you will need programming skills if you intend to do this yourself. However, most ISPs do not provide this sort of facility for non-business users. On the other hand, some ISPs provide a selection of basic scripts for any subscriber to use, including, typically, a search script and one for e-mailing the contents of a form. The ISP will provide some documentation about how to interface with such scripts. If you need this sort of facility, make sure you choose an ISP that offers it.

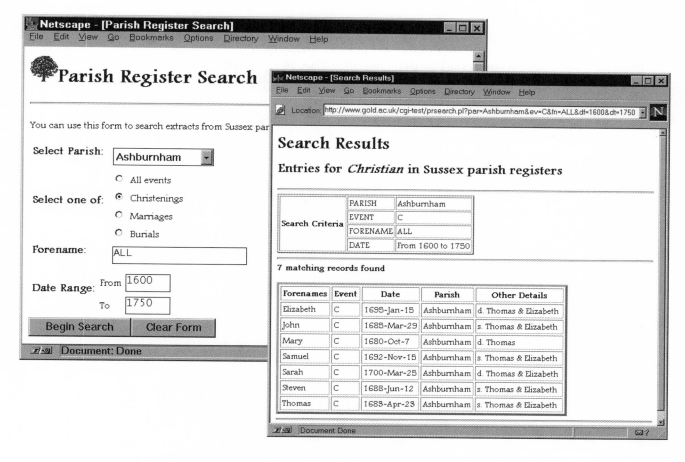

Fig. 17: Searching Parish Register Transcripts

The Parish Register Search page (*http://homepages.gold.ac.uk/peter/genealogy/prsearch.htm*) allows you to specify which records you are looking for. Clicking on **Begin Search** will submit the form to the server for processing. A CGI script then generates a Search Results page containing the selected records.

A further possibility is to use Microsoft's FrontPage. This can create pages which, when run on a FrontPage server, are able to exploit the server's script facilities without further ado. Again, though, ISPs only seem to provide FrontPage servers for business customers and at a greater cost than normal Web space. So this is not likely to be of use for personal Web pages, though if you are planning a site for a society, it may be worth considering.

But if all you want to do is help people find their way around your Web site, then you don't really need a search facility. If your Web site is well organized, i.e. it is clearly structured and each page provides clear navigational information, then a table of contents such as those on the GENUKI server or the Society of Genealogists Web site is likely to be more than adequate.[52] Don't forget, too, that once you have submitted your URL to the search engines, these will provide an index for you, and people will come to your Web site knowing there are pages which are potentially relevant to their interests.

In the future, however, we can expect to see database software developing features to support searching on the Web.

JAVASCRIPT

Many small scale interactive effects on Web pages are achieved by a simple programming language called **JavaScript**. This was designed specifically for the Web and, unlike CGI scripts, which run on the server, the JavaScript is contained in the text of the Web page it relates to. It therefore does not depend on what your ISP will support. While the idea of programming part of your Web page might seem rather daunting, borrowing small pieces of JavaScript and adapting them to your own needs is a lot simpler than learning to write CGI scripts.

JAVA

While JavaScript is only intended for small scale interactivity, **Java** is a fully fledged programming language for the Web, and can be used to write entire applications (called **applets**), from a Web-based calculator to an on-line shop or banking service. In contrast to JavaScript, you are not likely to be able to use Java unless you have (or are prepared to gain) considerable programming skills. And though in the future it may be possible to put ready-made Java applets (a search facility, for example) on a personal Web site, at present using Java is practicable only for Web authors with a programming background.

Frames

One feature you will see on many Web sites is the use of **frames** to break the screen up into a number of panels. Typically, these provide a page heading and a list of contents, which stay constant in their own areas of the screen, while different pages appear in a main panel depending on which item in the list of contents you select (see, for example, Fig. 4, p. 29). The advantage for the reader is that the list of con-

---

[52] *http://www.genuki.org.uk/mindex.html* and *http://www.sog.org.uk/map.html*, respectively. The latter was initially created automatically in FrontPage and then modified by hand.

tents remains on screen, making it easier to go to another area of the Web site. A number of HTML tools provide assistance in the creation of frame-based Web pages, and there is reference material available, though the interaction between the various panels on screen makes frame-based sites harder to design, and you may need to devote considerable time to experimenting.§

However, before you invest a lot of time and effort in learning how to create frame-based pages, you should note two disadvantages they have for your visitors:

❏ Unless well-thought-out and implemented, they can be confusing for readers.
❏ They may display very poorly for those with small screen resolutions such as the 640x480 typical of older Macs and PCs.

This really means that if you want to use frames, you should consider providing a set of pages without frames as well. To be honest, for personal genealogy pages, there is no compelling reason to use frames, but they can be useful as a way of simplifying the navigation of larger sites.

Controlling Access

There is very little reason why most family historians would want to restrict access to their Web sites, but both family history organizations and professional genealogists might find this useful, whether for chargeable access to transcripts and indexes, or to sell published materials. At the moment, with Web commerce still in its infancy, there are not yet straightforward systems in place for individuals and small organizations to collect small amounts of money via the Web, and many users are still rather cautious about paying for anything via the Internet (though it is demonstrably less open to fraud than many other financial transactions). However, this situation can be expected to change as Web commerce matures, and so cut out the labor and the time-lag of existing post office traces, and offer another way of selling publications.

It is also possible to provide restricted access to Web pages, and thus allow only members or those who have already paid for so many searches in advance to view the materials. Since this is usually done by protecting certain files or directories with passwords (sometimes via a form), it can only be done in consultation with your ISP, and, again, this facility is not something non-corporate users should expect as a matter of course.

Organizations and business users who want to implement such a system will need to discuss with their ISP whether such a facility is available before looking at the issues of how the system is implemented and maintained, and what it will cost. Some thought would need to be given to the technical aspects of any implementation:

❏ Who is going to keep the list of permitted users and passwords up to date?
❏ How do you make sure someone doesn't download your whole database?
❏ How do you stop someone from giving access to others who are not entitled?

You would certainly need specialist technical advice to get such a facility up and running, and if you are providing database searching, then database expertise will also be necessary.

If you want your visitors to be able to make purchases from your Web site, whether it is for physical items such as books or for access to databases and information, then you will need to have access to a secure server in order to guarantee the confidentiality of credit card information. Again, you will need to ensure that you place your account with an ISP that provides these facilities, and you will need to recruit or hire someone with suitable expertise.

Appendices

A. Glossary

Attribute An optional addition to an HTML *tag* which modifies what the tag does.

Bookmark The record of a Web page's title and Web address kept by a browser in a *bookmark list*. Users can add to the bookmark list any pages they want to remember.

Browser The software that is used to view Web pages. A graphical browser can display images, a text-only browser cannot.

CGI Common Gateway Interface. A standard way of passing data entered by a reader into a Web form. The data is usually handled by a *script*.

Client The computer of the person accessing the Internet, or the software being used to retrieve information from a *server*.

Compression A technique for making files smaller so that they can be downloaded more quickly.

Converter A program that converts a document from one file format into another; also called a *filter*.

Download To copy data from a central server to an individual user's computer.

Filter See *converter*.

Form Part of a Web page with areas the reader can fill in or select options from. The information is then passed to the server for processing.

Freeware Software which can be freely distributed and used without payment to the author. Also called Public Domain Software.

FTP File Transfer Protocol, the standard method of uploading and downloading files on the Internet.

GEDCOM The standard format for the interchange of genealogical data.

GIF A standard graphics file format supported by all graphical Web browsers.

Home Page The main entry point to a Web site.

Hot Spot A piece of text or an image on a Web page that causes the browser to fetch a different page when selected (usually by clicking with the mouse). The hot spot is usually highlighted in some way to indicate that it can be selected.

HTML	HyperText Markup Language. This defines what can and can't appear on Web pages.
ISP	Internet Service Provider; also called Internet Access Provider.
Identifier	The essential part of a *tag* which indicates which tag it is.
Image Map	Any graphic image that can cause different pages to be loaded by the browser, depending on which part of the image the reader selects.
In-Line Graphic	A graphic that appears as part of a Web page.
Java	A programming language used for dynamic Web pages.
JavaScript	A scripting language used for dynamic Web pages.
JPEG	A graphics file format supported by an increasing number of Web browsers, particularly suited to photographic quality images.
Link	A connection between two Web pages, indicated by a *hot spot*.
Markup	Adding marks to a text to indicate how it should be presented; in HTML these marks are called *tags*.
On-line Service	A service that provides its own discussion-groups, file archives and mail facilities, and which nowadays also provides access to the Internet.
Pathname	The complete specification of where a file is located on a disk, including the filename and the directory/folder names.
PNG	Portable Network Graphics, an image format designed specifically for the Web, though not currently widely used.
RTF	A file format for word-processed documents readable by many different computers and word-processors, and which preserves a large amount of formatting information; stands for Rich Text Format.
Script	A computer program that deals with data entered on a Web form.
Server	The central computer, which provides data when it receives requests from a *client*. Servers are generally fast machines with large amounts of disk space, able to cope with many different requests at once.
Shareware	Software that can be freely distributed and evaluated for a limited period (often 30 days), after which the user is expected to register the software by paying a license fee.
Source	The plain text HTML file that defines what will appear on a Web page. A browser retrieves the *source* from a server and turns it into the displayed page. Most browsers allow you to see the source for a page you are viewing.
Style Sheet	A mechanism for separating the presentation of a Web page from the structure of its information. A style sheet is linked to a page it applies to.

Tag	An *identifier* between angled brackets, used singly or in pairs to indicate to the browser how various features of a Web page should be displayed.
Thumbnail	A small version of an image used to link to a larger version.
Upload	To copy data from an individual user's computer to a central server.
URL	Uniform Resource Locator. The standard method of referring to any Internet resource. The URL of a Web page is its "address."
Validation	The checking of an HTML file to establish whether it conforms to published standards; a way of detecting HTML errors in Web pages.
Virtual Server	A Web site that has its own *server* name, even though in fact it is just an area on a larger server.
Web Server	A *server* dedicated to providing Web pages.
Web Site	A group of Web pages that form a coherent unit.
Wizard	A software facility which guides the user through a series of steps to simplify some otherwise complex process.
W3C	The World Wide Web Consortium, which controls the HTML standard.

B. Recommended Books & Articles

There are countless books on Web publishing available. However, those published before 1997 will not have reliable coverage of HTML 4.0, the current standard, or new features like cascading style sheets. However, you will also find many books about Web design or more general issues such as Web graphics, and these don't date nearly as quickly. Short books which just list the features of HTML or give lists of tags are not worth the money — this information is free on the Web if it's not in your Web authoring software. My own recommendation would be:

> Laura Lemay & Arman Danesh, *Teach Yourself Web Publishing with HTML 4 in a Week* (Sams, 1997).

General computer magazines and those specifically devoted to the Internet regularly have articles on Web publishing, as well as reviews of Web publishing software.

There is not yet much in print on specifically genealogical uses of the Web and recent books on Internet genealogy have paid scant attention to Web publishing, but *Genealogical Computing* regularly covers this area.

An overview of GEDCOM converters is provided by Alan Mann's "From GEDCOM to a Web Page" in *Genealogical Computing* Vol. 18, No. 1 (Summer 1998).

C. Getting Web Software

All shareware or freeware Web software can be downloaded from the Web. With commercial packages, you will often find a demo on the company's Web site. You will frequently find Web authoring software on cover CDs of computer magazines and accompanying books on Web authoring. CD-ROMs are useful because of the very substantial download times required for some of the fuller packages.

Windows and Mac users looking for software should look at the lists provided on the TUCOWS Web site (*http://www.tucows.com/*)[53], which has a good rating system, brief descriptions of the software, and has the software available for downloading from a selection of servers for every geographical region. TUCOWS is also useful because it rates packages and in some cases offers reviews. Other reviews will be found on the Web pages of computer magazines.

Otherwise the best general starting point for any Web software is on Yahoo (*http://www.yahoo.com/*). All material relating to the Web and Web authoring is available from the page *http://www.yahoo.com/Computers_and_Internet/Internet/World_Wide_Web/*.

CompuServe users can find some of the specifically genealogical software in the Internet Genealogy Library (Lib 20) of the Genealogy Forum, while the Internet Resources Forum has a library for general WWW/Hypertext Tools.

D. On-line Resources

There are an enormous number of resources on the Web relating to Web authoring: the Web site for this book (*http://www.walrus.dircon.co.uk/wpg/*) contains many of the examples used in the text or links to them, as well as links to a variety of resources for the areas discussed in this book

On the other hand, there is relatively little on the Web specifically about creating genealogical Web sites. Cyndi's List (*http://www.cyndislist.com/*) lists relevant software and provides a tutorial under the title "Genealogy Home Page Construction Kit" at *http://www.CyndisList.com/construc.htm*. Mark Howells' article "Transforming your GEDCOM Files into Web Pages" is available at *http://www.oz.net/~markhow/writing/gedcom.htm*. Other related articles by Mark are listed at *http://www.oz.net/~cyndihow/*.

Two essential sites for anyone interested in GEDCOM converters are Mark Knight's page at *http://www.pinn.net/~knightma/*, which shows sample output for most current converters, and the Surname Web's list of converters, with reviews of several of them at *http://surnameweb.org/help/conversion.htm*.

There are also a number of newsgroups devoted to the Web, and specifically to Web editing, authoring and publishing, notably *comp.infosystems.www.authoring.html* and *comp.infosystems.www.authoring.images*, while *soc.genealogy.computing* discusses all issues relating to computers and genealogy. There is a useful page on "What newsgroups discuss the Web?" at *http:/sunsite.unc.edu/boutell/faq/ngroups.htm*.

---

[53] The URL given is for the main TUCOWS site — check for the mirror site nearest to you, in order to get the best download times.

Index